LIKE A HANDKERCHIEF GIRL

Memoirs of a girl

aspiring to be,

to see,

and

to live,

embracing life

by

M. Virginia Southworth

for

Mom

and

also,

for

Mr. Cembalski

To Virginia

On Her Birthday

Your past is past and never to return,

The long bright yesterday of life's first years,

Its days are dead --- cold ashes in an urn.

Some, held for you a chalice for your tears,

And other days strewed flowers upon your way.

They are all gone beyond my speech

I know them not, so that your first gone times

To me unknown, lie far beyond my rhymes.

But I can bless your soul and aims today,

And I can ask your future to be sweet,

And I can pray that you may never meet

With any cross, you are too weak to bear.

Virginia, virgin name, and may you wear

its virtues and its beauties, fore'er and fore'er.

I breathe this blessing, and I pray this prayer.

Father Abram J. Ryan, 1880

PART I

Like a Handkerchief Girl

Little Virginia

Born into large family in a small Adirondack town was "Little Virginia", the sixth of twelve children. There were four boys and eight girls though the last child did not arrive until Virginia was seventeen.

Virginia was named after her mother who was named after her aunt - Great Aunt Virginia. At that time, babies were birthed in the home. However, a new hospital had been built and the Farleigh family being a prominent family deemed it best to show their support for the new hospital. Hence great-Aunt Virginia gave birth to a baby boy in the hospital. She had contracted an infection and tragically died shortly after. Her beautiful portrait hangs in the parlor at the big house. The "big house" is a large stone house next door to where the Audette family lived. The Audette family lived in the old Sheridan Farleigh house on Champlain Avenue.

Ticonderoga is an Indian name meaning "between two lakes". This town is stiuated between Lake George and Lake Champlain nestled in the foot of the Adirondack Mountains.

Perhaps Virginia's earliest memory, is that of her two older sisters telling her to go potty having removed the bowl from the potty chair.

Central School

Virginia was a painfully shy child - so quiet was she tht the kindergarten teacher, Mrs. Robinson, threatened to mark her absent if she did not speak up to announce she was "here" when the teacher was taking attendance. One boy, Michael Sullivan, would always confidently declare, "Present!" when his name was called. Little Virginia was so shy that she never got the chance or dared to ask if she could ride the tricycle - a regret that has never left her. It also irked hr that Joe Wallace sat on the edge of one of her art projects - which tore the corner. He was also the same one who dominated the tricycle. She did, however, enjoy the 'Merry-go-round' which was on the Portage side of the playground. She also enjoyed when hermother would send in those pink frosted cookies and Hi-C punch for various holiday parties. At the Christmas party, Virginia reached into the grab bag and with one eye open, plucked the very gift that he had brought in. It was a coloring book and crayons. She loved to draw and this was a sure thing. One of the assistants in Mrs. Robinson's class, a Mrs. Duprey, used to come in and read to the children. She was a large lady and, peculiarly, she would drape her dress over the back of the small wooden chair when she sat down. There was a glory day for the the young girl on the last day of kindergarten. Mrs. Robinson presented Virginia with a red crown made from construction paper. A dime was taped in the center of it. She received this because her birthday was in the summer. All the children would get one for their birthday. The child proudly donned her crown as she paraded down Champlain Avenue to her nearby family's stucco house.

There were many comings and goings at the Central School besides there being a monument out front commemorating British General Lord Howe. There were clinits set up for Polio shots. The Voting polls took place there. There were Friday night dances for the teen crowd. When school was in session in the 1960's, there were bomb raid drills in addition to the fire drills. Those metal stairways were on the side of the building going up to the roof. Virginia and her brothers used to run up them. Only one time, they left their sister up there and they ran off. Then they would play out front on the big swing set. There was this one fellow, named George

LaDue. It was said that he was swinging so high and so fast thathe flung right over the swing set itself!

The neat thing about this school is that is it the very school that Virginia's grandfather attended. An old maid school teacher often commented on how Grampa still had those mischievous brown eyes even into his late eighties.

Right across from the school there was a big grey house with green trim. It had a sprawling porch. Virginia and her brother Thomas used to play house here. They would have homemade tea parties. Thomas was the made-up name of "Megowil" and Virginia called herself "Aunt Alcohol". It is a wonder tht the owners never came home and caught them. This, of course, never occurred to these two children.

Then, the twosome would traipse down to the nearby army building. There they would climb into these huge army tanks out back and play in them. Interestingly enough, Virginia does not care for closed -in places.

These were the days when "Honey" McCoy would come in adn help take care of the Audette children. Honey and Don McCoy lived on the Trout Brook Road in South Ticonderoga. Honey's hands always smelled of bleach as she was always cleaning. She was an excellent cook and baker. She prided herself on the fact that her husband Don could always tell the difference if she baked a cake from a box mix or from scratch. Honey would boune Tisdale, the youngest at that time, on her lap and sing, "Tisdale is a little brown berry, Tisdale is, a little brown berry ..." Honey was a kind and maternal woman. She would let the Audette children come out and spend the night in the countryside where she lived. Her son Davey would give the kids piggy back rides. Virginia was especially intrigued by the metal register plate that was vented for the warm air to come through upstairs. Little Virginia got to pick pussy willows and "cat tails" which she proudly brought into school when she was in the second grade. On those days, she would get up early and ride the bus in from Tuffertown to school with the McCoy children.

St. Mary's

While Virginia's older brothers and sisters attended St. Mary's School, Virginia would take her younger brother and the four little girls over to the school. They would peer in the windows to see if they could see one of their older siblings. One boy in Annie's class named Robert would announce, "There are the Audette-ies!" Then Sister Bethany would come out and tell the children to run along.

It was when little Virginia was in first grade that her maternal great-grandmother died. She left school early and proceded to take a large can of beans from the cupboard. She was standing on a chair reaching for them when Daddy had told her to go next door to the big house as there was lots of food there. Virginia was thinkingof Nana Farleigh and the time that Nana wsa putting the potatoes and onions on her plate. Her hands were arthritic and they frightened the young child. She was not able to eat the onions. Yet Nana wsa the kindest, most generous soul who looked out for the lonely and those who had fallen on hard times. Even if they had no money, Nana took them in. There was a man who lived at the big house. He used to be a watch maker. His name was Arthur. He had snow white hair. He used to come around the children making a buzzing sound pretending that he was going to "sting" them. The kids called him "The Bumblebee". Thomas was especially scared of him. He would hide behind the loveseat in the parlor.

Nana was laid out in the library of the big house. Mr. O'Malley across the way was watching people coming and going in the big house. She shouted from across the street, "Who died?"

First Grade

Sister Mary Mark taught Virginia in the First grade. The nuns were very good to the Audette family. They gave them free lunches at school. Only Virginia was unsure of this so she went home for lunch on the first day. One time Virginia was stumbling on a problem that had the word 'several' in it. She figured they must have meant 'seven'. She did manage to get the correct answer. One girl in the class asked Virginia to ride the bus home with her. She lived on Warner Hill Road next to an apple orchard. Her name was Christine. Virginia was too shy to tell her 'no'. Later, Christine's father brought Virginia back home with a bag of apples in tow.

It was a very special day in May when the youngster made her First Holy Communion. She received that pretty white vinyl pocketbook that smelled like the new dolls she and her sisters got at Christmas. Inside was a prayer book, the scapular, a Miraculous Medal and a little white set of Rosary beads. She wore the pretty white dress and veil that her two older sisters wore. She had new white shoes with pretty little lace anklets. What ws foremost in the girl's mind was something she was unprepared for. One of the classmates Marta Aiello spat out the Sacred Host. Little Virginia knew right where It was. When Gramma Farleigh was getting ready to take her to the Fort, Virginia told her about it. Gramma Farleigh was greatly disturbed as she is a devout Catholic. Poor Marta was not quite right. Grandmother summoned the priest and Virginia showed them right where It was. Then Gramma took the child to the Fort in her 1960's white Falcon car. They sat in the tall pine chairs at the soda fountain where her father and grandfather were working. Virginia had a hot chocolate and she felt very important on that very special day.

She would ride with her grandmother on many an occasion in that white car going up Black Point Road to visit great Uncle Tom. Gramma would make a point to stop at the Corner Market and let little Virginia pick out a treat. She would pick out those large square marshmallows covered in toasted coconut. Annie would select the orange marshmallow peanuts. Uncle Tom had a dog named 'Midnight'. He never refrigerated his condiments. He was quite a character in his own right. One time he was walking down Black Point Road and Mr. Whitstone offered him a ride. A dog was close by and they both proceded to get in the car. Uncle Tommy got out and Mr. Whitstone said, "Don't forget your dog - " and Uncle Tom replied, "Not my dog."

What goes through the minds of children. Little Virginia asked her grandmother which she would prefer on her car - a bunch of spiders, or a bunch of snakes? "I don't think I would care to have either." Gramma replied.

At the end of first grade, Sister Mary Mark gave little Virginia this pretty white 'Pieta' statue. However, a classmate named Maria liked this and she offered her pencil in exchange for it. Virginia did not really want to trade, but she obliged.

Second Grade

The principal would scan over all the students when the bell rang to make sure they were dressed properly. One cool Autumn day, Virginia was sent home to get a sweater. She returned home and came back with one of her mother's sweaters. It was a beautiful cardigan from Iceland. It had a lovley pattern iwth olive greens and browns and a little rust color in it. Her father had been stationed in Reykjavik when he was in the Air Force. He brought this back for Virginia's mother.

Virginia was in the "Brownies" when she was eight years old. She was permitted to wear her Brownie uniform to school on Thursdays as she had her Brownie meetings after school in the nearby Armory building. She took great pride in her uniform. She would iron it in the morning before school. She would also iron her father's shirts for which he would give her a dime for her dues. One time, she got carried awaw with the iron and she pressed her leotards. They stuck to the iron.

At Halloween time, Sister Jean Marie asked if anyone had any perishables. Virginia had brought in a bag of 'Three Musketeers'. She was not sure if they were perishable or not, so she raised her hand. Then Sister said, "Those are not perishable."

During a math equation involving fractions, Virginia happened to get the right answer. Sister Jean Marie went to the clothes cupboard and pulled out a jawbreaker from her stash. The child was rewarded and then asked to explain how she came about her answer. She was afraid to tell her that it was just a lucky guess.

One girl in the second grade, Emily Angelo, always had her box of 64 Crayola Crayons sitting on her desk. It was the kind that had the built-in crayon sharpener. Most of the students had the 8-pack while a few had the 24 -pack. Virginia loved art and she liked to draw. There was a contest to draw a turtle. The librarian was giving away a book that had the Caldecott medal. It was a toss-up between Virginia and David Macio, but the book went to David.

Then came a very sad day in the second grade. One classmate suffered from the lung disease Cystic Fibrosis. We had just learned that her younger sister in the first grade died from the same disease. Virginia overheard Sister saying to the parents that their daughter was no longer suffering. Virginia went to the wake with her mother. She knelt before what appeared to be an angel with blonde hair - wearing lbue velvet - so frail, "Please wake up...." the child prayed.

Little Mary was in the hospital with Pneumonia when she was five years old. When she came home, the nuns were on hand to visit and see how she was doing. They gave Mary a little nun statue. For all Mother had on her mind, she did things very nicely. She picked up some pink marshmallow cookies that had coconut on them. She served lemonade in the light blue ceramic pitcher that had pretty flowers on it. They were set on a coffee table in front of the fireplace. The fireplace had those unusual wrought andirons. They resembled fairies but they were masculine with tall slender hats. The only other ones that Virginia has since seen are at Ellen and Jim Hebert's house on Chilson Hill. On the mantle, was a beautiful Louis XVI gold gilt clock. Heavy bronze candlesticks that had a lily flourish to them stood on either side of the mantle.

The children could not wait for the nuns to leave as they could have the "leavings" as one Mima Bennett used to say.

Little Virginia - 1967

Virginia's father was working at the historical Fort Ticonderoga at the time. Her mother taught Latin at the school in Mineville a couple of towns over. Her mother always kept a stash of Hershey bars in her second dresser drawer. She would take one to school every week to give to this one handicapped boy. This had always made an impression on the young girl. Another thing that Virginia fondly remembered, was that if her mother was running late for school, and one of the kids could not find a matching sock, her mother would take the time to sift through a bag until shoe dound one suitable. One these same mornings, Grampa would bring in the freshly laundered clothes still warm from the Sunshine Corners Laundromat dryer. He helped out doing the laundry for the family and he would open the Laundromat for the owner bright and early. Usually, the oldest girl, Lizzy, would go through the basket first. She would also go through the pack of individual cereal boxes quick to pick out the "Special K' or the "Raisin Bran". Thomas likes the Sugar Pops and little Virginia invariably ended up with the corn flakes. The children would sit at the built-in breakfast nook. Daddy would come around and give a nuzzle to everyone before leaving for the Fort.

The Big House

If she was not eating corn flakes at "303", her older sisters would be putting the kettle over to boil next door at the "big house" where Gramma Farleigh lived. Only, Virginia would rise shortly before the church bell rang and go over to the church behind the house and sit with Gramma Farleigh at daily Mass.

Lizzy was fair with thick blonde and blue eyes and Annie had dark hair and brown eyes; everyone said that Annie resembled great Aunt Virginia. The two older sisters would get out the rice crispies, the bread for toast and the oranges on any given day back at 307 Champlain Avenue. Then does not one learn to live by one's wits in a large family. Virginia would proudly re-use her tea bag several times trying to impress her grandmother who responded, "I think you like hot water."

Uncle H.G., mother's brother, called the younger sister trailing behind the two older ones "Little Sister". Little Sister took note of how Uncle H.G. put peanut butter on his toast. Aunt Betty would butter the corners of her toast and then dot butter in the center.

Little Virginia had a unique style. She has always liked that crisp, military look. Before she started at St.Mary's, she wanted to copy everything that her oldest brother Georgie did. Georgie wore navy blue pants to school so Little Virginia had to have a pair like her brother's. This use to irk her oldest sister. But her oldest sister was the best big sister. She was fiercely protective of her younger brothers and sisters. One time, Karlene, one of the four little girls as they were affectionately referred, had her birthday money stolen at the shopping mall in Glens Falls. Karlene had set it down in the restroom and this woman took it. Lizzy confronted her and layed her out in lavender, but Karlene never got her money back.

Speaking of laying out in lavender, when Karlene, the second youngest "little girl", came running from the back porch of the big house. She was screaming that she saw Nana. Of course this was after Nana had died. Karlene could not have been more than four years old. She described Nana's lavender dress with pearl buttons and a brooch that which she was wearing when she was laid to rest.

Nana had a white cat. The white cat ended up in Plattsburgh, New York. His name was, "White Cat". White Cat made its way back to Ticonderoga.

Another eerie thing associated with Nana was when her best friend Clara died. The night before, Nana was lying in bed in the downstairs bedroom at the big house. Clara drifted past her bedroom window and said, "Good bye Mrs. Farleigh." This has become a catch phrase among the Audette children. It has been repeated, dramatized and mocked over the years sometimes with extra syllables added and proclaimed in a "haunting" fashion.

The Big House

Mrs. O'Malley across the street had a loud, piercing voice. One could always hear her respond in church, "And With Your Spirit!"

Virginia had a penchant for striped shirts. Not just one, but she would layer many - one on top of another sometimes wearing four or five shirts at once. She also wore a red baseball cap everywhere she went. She was, afterall, between two brothers growing up. She loved what they liked and that meant baseball. She was actually quite good at baseball. She was good at hitting and catching the ball. She was also a very fast runner. Her brothers and sisters would play whiffle ball in the side yard or soft ball, volley ball or kick ball. They would also play badminton, or croquet. Aunt Arthurlyn and Uncle Tommy gave the family a croquet set one Christmas.

Third Grade

Third Grade, upstairs classroom facing Amherst Avenue, Sister Maurice was the teacher. REd hair showed under her wimple. Virginia was very scared of her. She always had that yardstick in her hand and she would threaten to use it if one's homework was not done. One day, she could not find Virginia's homework which Virginia had handed in. She was getting ready to put her hand out when the Saints came through, and her paper manifested. She returned to her seat. There was, however, a most embarrassing incident for the youngster. Bathroom privileges were at appointed times. So Virginia did not dare ask when she felt the urge to go one day. She tried with all her might to hold it in, bu it was of little use. Then, the nun approached her. She told her to go home and get cleaned up. It was the child's first real lesson in humility. Her brother Thomas had been home sick from school. He asked his sister why she was home early. "Sister said I stink." came the reply as Virginia drew a bath. Aside from that, Virginia learned multiplication and she was adept at cursive. Spelling came easy to her. She was confounded by the way Sister Maurice made her 'r's though. They connected strangely like a cross between an 'n' and a 'v'. Virginia concluded that this must be the way the nun makes her 'r's.

One other thing confounded Virginia in the third grade. Sister was talking about 'black magic'. She said that she could do some but only one student in the classroom was privy to how this worked. Karen Grady was brought outside the classroom. When she came back in, she somehow, mysteriously knew the answers to certain questions. Virginia often wondered about this.

Virginia's favorite book in the third grade was "Mr. Popper's Penguins".

One time when little Virginia was not much more than eight years of age, she found a dime on the cellar floor where her father had his "mancave". It was a dark Sunday night and a school night at that. That did not stop the child from walking down to bevilacqua's candy store and buying a pack of cinnamon red hots. Since it was a busy household, she went and came back unnoticed.

One thing that sticks in Virginia's mind from Saint Mary's, is the smell of oil from the boiler room. The thrid grade classroom was above the boiler room. Christine's uncle was the janitor there. He was also a farmer like Christine's dad. Virginia's oldest brother Georgie used to help "Johnny" as he was affectionally called. Bobby Bush, also nicknamed 'Shrubs', helped out too. Johnny gave Georgie the family's first dog - Wilbur, a beagle. Wilbur went everywhere where the Audette family went including to Mass and he would be close to the Communion Rail. Wilbur was a real smart dog and yes, he was Catholic.

Her brother Henry stayed back so he was in third grade with his sister. He and Bobby Shumaker were always up to mischief. Throw tony Bevilacqua into the mix and there was a real crew. But Bobby Schumaker could sing. For music, he sang "America the Beautiful." To this day, when Virginia hears that song, she thinks of Bobby Shumaker.

Fourth Grade

Sister Bertha taught fourth grade at St. Mary's. This was when the school uniforms changed. They went from the Royal blue jumpers with a split front bodice, white blouse and blue bow tie - ribbon style and beanies to the plaid jumper with white 'Peter Pan' collar The mothers voted on this.

The nuns were very good to the Audette family. They saw to it that they had their lunches taken care of. A typical lunch might be Spanish rice, green beans, roll and butter, milk and maybe a dish of pears for dessert. There would be spaghetti and meat balls, with St. Mary's trademark chocolate brownies for dessert. They were dusted with powdered sugar. Another day might feature "Pennies from Heaven" with prunes for dessert. There would be tomato soup and grilled cheese sandwiches on a Friday, sometimes pizza which was always popular; meat with brown gravy over mashed potatoes on another day or baked chicken the next. They were wholesome and hearty. One day, Virginia's younger sister Mary came home from school and she announced that Susan Henthorn put her finger in her hash. It is funny the things that one never forgets.

Sister Bertha had a soft spot for young Virginia. She was an older nun. If you were to do a word or song association with this sister, it would, hands down be "The King of Glory". The class was always singing that song/hymn. It was right before Spring break and shortly after Easter when she summoned the girl to her desk after school. She presented her with a large brown paper bag that had this big bread with bits of lemon in it and icing on it with sprinkles on top. It must have been an Easter bread. It was wrapped in foil. Virginia shared it with her brother Thomas and their imaginary friends, 'Megowil' and "Aunt Alcohol". They ate it under the trees between the big house and the Episcopal church. It was pretty to look at if hard to bite.

The students attended Mass on First Fridays, and other special Feast Days. May Crownings were very special. but sadly, many of these beautiful traditons died out as Vatican II was ushered in. Virginia remembers sitting with her mother in church when Mass was in Laatin. Her mother always had, a tissue in her pocket, a couple of saltines, a mint and some lipstick.

Halloween

It was always a treat going to the convent on Halloween. You could catch a glimpse of the table set for the next meal in the dining room. The cream colored dishes had a little gold design on them. There was a turquoise color inside the china cups. The set came from the "five and dime" store. The cups were placed upside down on their saucers - that which always intrigued little Virginia. And then there were napkin rings. Each Sister had her own personalized napkin ring. To this day, Virginia loves her napkin rings. Well, then Sisters gave out popcorn balls wrapped in cellophane. Go up Father Jogues Place a little farther and the Royces would give you and apple. The priests had large candy bars at the rectory. One older woman who lived alone on top of Champlain Avenue gave out chocolate sandwich cookies. If a house forgot it was Halloween, one might et a nickel or the lights would be turned off. Halloween was a fun time for the Audette family. They would come back with a big grocery store bag loaded with candy and treats. They would stay up late eating a good portion of their larder.

Perhaps the best treats of all, were the French pastries that Grampa and Daddy brought back from their trips to Montreal. There would be custard filled pastries in assorted colors and shapes: pink elephants, lady bugs and butterflies. They were the stuff dreams are made of - covered in fresh cream and chocolate and garnished with strawberries. They were in a large white cardboard box and they were kept in the ice box. Everyone enjoyed them!!

Probably all those treats led to the many visits to the nearby dentist. Mother was sure to see that the children took care of their teeth. Virginia had a thorough teeth cleaning when she was nine years old. She was very impressed with that red tablet and learning about flossing. She also acquired a mouth full of mercury silver fillings. However, she was scrupulous from then on with her dental hygiene.

Gramma and Little Virginia coming from Mass

Christmastime

The students exchanged names at Christmas for gift giving. While "The Book of Lifesavers candy" are good, they were also the kind of predictable gift that the kids would prefer not to get. Virginia had this one girl's name - Roseanne. Roseanne was very popular. Virginia wanted to impress her by not giving her the stanard book of Lifesavers. She went to Meyer's drugstore.There was a pretty statue of a little girl holding a kitten. It was perfect. It cost more than the candy would have, but it was on sale. She left the store on this winter evening delighted with her purchase. 'Lo and behold, when she got behind the 'Save Way' store, it slipped out of her hands and fell to the pavement - breaking! So much for trying to impress. Roseanne got lifesavers afterall, but she was a gracious girl so it was alright. Virginia received bath beads from a classmate named Jean. Meanwhile, Virginia's older sister Annie, gave a black mantilla to Lynn Riola. This girl was not happy with it. Today,mantillae are very hard to find and then dear at that.

"I'll give you a dime for your pork chop Henry," Annie would barter. It was all good though because there were so many. It meant that there were twelve Freihofer round birthday cakes to look forward to throughout the year. These were always accompanied by a gallon of coffee ice cream.

Christmas was even better. All the aunts and uncles contributed to make sure the family had lots of presents. There would be a family toboggan, board games, new skis, ice skates, new winter coats and boots; a foot ball or a baseball glove. One year, there was a huge tray of great big juicy seedless oranges. The tag said it was for "Virginia". Little Virginia always craved oranges - perhaps it was due to the long winters in the North Country. She was very excited when she saw them and even happier to share them. As she grew older, it dawned on her, that they really must have been meant for her mother of the same name. They were from Gramma and Grampa Audette. With her mother in the motherly way most of the time, fresh fruit would have been good for her. In fact, Christine teRiele's father always made sure mother had liver. He was a farmer. Gramma Farleigh always got the family a huge box of the most delicious Empire apples. Virginia would never forget the first time she bit into one of these. Even though it was fruit, it satisfied her as much as if it were chocolate cake.

Around Town

Virginia and her older sister Annie or her brother Thomas or Henry would regularly walk downtown to the candy store. It was run by an Italian family. Whatever change the kids had, they would buy "fire balls", "Good & Plenty", "Charleston Chews", "Baby Ruths", "Junior Mints", "Mallo Cups", Bazooka gum and maybe a Nehi Birch beer or a cream soda. Those bottles were worth two cents which meant more candy could be had the next day. One time Georgie bought a bottle of cola and there was a bobby pin in the bottom of the bottle. There was also the rumor that a grandmother of one of the classmate found a cockroach in her blueberry yogurt.

When Virginia would go to Bevilacqua's candy store with Thomas, they would time it right before the evening train would come through. Then, they would stand alongside of the train tracks, and watch all the train cars whiz by. They were mesmerized. They often felt transported and like they were taking a journey themselves. The train would go through several times a day to the old paper mill and beyond. One could hear the haunting sound of the train whistle in the early hours of the morning.

The Audettes would wake up to the sound of the church bells and then they would ring when it was lunch time and supper time - or more appropriately, for the Angelus.

The church and the school were literally in the backyard. Indeed the school is on Farleigh property which is rented for a dollar a year.

The Paternal SIde

Virginia's great grandparents on her father's side were from an old Boston family. Her great grandfather or "Boopa" as he was called by his grandchildren was a civil engineer. He was an integral part in the construction of the original Crown Point Bridge which spanned Lake Champlain from Crown Point to Chimney Point in Vermont. There was a plaque on the bridge which had his name on it. This was in the center of the bridge. Grandmother Audette christened the bridge in 1929 when she was just sixteen years old. FDR came and President Coolidge was on hand. There was a huge parade and quite a motorcade. FDR had a photograph sent to Mortimer Yale Ferris, (Boopa), in which he wrote on the "We can both agree that Miss Ferris is a very pretty young lady." Boopa's family were in the Oriental Trade during the mid-1800's. Great Grandmother's family, the Raymonds, were from a family of ship builders. When Boopa was dating Mam Mam, (great grandmother), he told her of his family's trading. Mam Mam reminded hinm of the ships that her family built to make the passages possible for the Trade. Anyway, Virginia's mother would stop on this bridge here on her way to Burlington, Vermont. Usually, it was to go to the hospital there as Thomas, Henry or Daddy were there at different times. It may have been for a family Christmas shopping venture where there was sure to be a stop at Seward's soda fountain for maple walnut ice cream.

Ingenuity of Karl

There was something in the backyard that used to spook the neighborhood kids. That was a gravestone of Great-Great Grandfather Farleigh. This was the original stone. However, it had been replaced with a newer one where he is buried in the family plot at Mount Hope Cemetery. Curious children would not be satisfied with that as a "digging" ensued - only to have worms for fishing! This stone, rounded at the top, was near the white swingset. The swingset that the family had was most unusual. There were ladders made of white metal going up and down on both sides. This was a good sturdy one unlike any other. The second oldest boy, Karl, devised a pulley that ran from the big house back porch down to the swingset. He had a seat made from wood on it and the little girls would get rides on it to and fro.

Behind the big house, there used to be a big wooden barn where a sleigh was kept. At one time, there were horses in there. Some neighborhood boys were playing in it with matches and a terrible fire ensued.

Another invention that Karl devised was a floating ghost in Gramma Farleigh's attic. He ran a string across the rafters and he had a long dress hanging from it with a hat above it. When the attic door opened, the ghost would float like Clara herself and screams would descend on the big house. Aunt Mary said that Gramma did not appreciate this, but boys will be boys. There was never a dull moment with the Audette children. They had great imaginations. They had each other and they looked out for each other.

Karl used to make these gas balloons out of Gramma Farleigh's dry cleaner bags and coat hanger wires. People were calling the radio station about a possible UFO sighting seen hovering over Saint Mary's School.

Karl would also get about eight of his brothers and sisters and they would all pile in the toboggan and slide down the hill behind the big house. He would also take the "Flexible Flyer" and lie on his stomach, Virginia on his back and they would fly down Champlain Avenue arriving at Walsh's corner.

Olaf

Olaf was mother's Great Dane that she got when she went away to college. He had a very commanding presence. He used to scratch the oak doors in the big house. One year, when the family was at mid-night Mass, Olaf ate the goose. The goose was not only cooked, it was gone! The priest would come to the big house and the neighbors. One man from Hague went to school in Ti, (short for Ticonderoga), and he stayed at the big house. His name was Gilette Bartlett. He had movie star looks and a personality to match. Another fellow, who did stay at the big house did become a movie star. That was Michael (Armstrong) Whitney. He was from Chilson. He was a big man - a sort of gentle giant. He was a terrific baseball player and athlete. Mother's brother, Uncle Tommy, was a great baseball player too. They played on a team on Chilson Hill. Michael Whitney was born Michael Armstrong. He played in a lot fo Western shows on TV. He was married to the British model Twiggy. They would come back to the big house to visit. Uncle H. G. would call up for little Virginia to meet Twiggy. Her accent was delightful! Virginia got her autograph and some pointers on how to be a movie star which was her aspiration. Whitney suggested that she get involved with summer stock theater.

Great Aunt Lacrecia

Great Aunt Lacrecia would visit at the big house. She was Nana's daughter same as great Aunt Virginia was. Aunt Lacrecia had three sons - two of whom were a set of twins. One time, little Virginia was using the big bathroom at the big house when Aunt Lacrecia accidentally came in. Little Virginia was sitting on the throne. Aunt Lacrecia apologized. She was wearing a brocade dress that had turquoise and green colors.

Mother would take the Audette children to visit Great Aunt Lacrecia in Whitehall. The new road was being put in during the 1960's. Aunt Lacrecia lived above a little store. She would give the children a few dimes to buy some candy.

Mother's youngest brother and sibling is Uncle Sherry. Sherry was a lot of fun. He used to give "airplane rides' hoisting the little Audette children on his feet while lying on the library floor in the big house. He used to have a hard time waking up in the morning. Gramma Farleigh would tell the children to wake up their Uncle Sherry with a pail of water. Later, he taught little Virginia how to make lasagna. He was a great cook. He also served his country in the Army.

Another fun thing the kids did at the big house, was to take the prisms off the gold gilt chandelier mantle decorations above the green tile fireplace in the library. They would walk around staring into them filled with an array of rainbow colors and wonder. They would also rub their stocking feet on the Oriental rugs and go around surprising each other with shocks of static electricity.

Tang was the drink being touted back then. There was always a big jar of Tang at the big house. There was a spice tea recipe that incorporated Tang in it too.

In the Summer of 1969 the family all sat around the black and white TV to see Apollo 11 land on the moon. It was very exciting. On July 20th, when the Lunar Model landed. A few hours later, on July 21st, Buzz Aldrin set foot on the Moon! Twenty minutes later, Neil Armstrong joined him.

Speaking of "Buzz" and electricity, Virginia's two older sisters Annie and Lizzy used to give Virginia a butter knife and tell the Virginia to put it in the electrical outlet. Then, loudly, they would shout, "B-B-B- BUZZZZ!

Odd Jobs

Saturdays were relegated to cleaning the big house for Gramma Farleigh. Annie and Lizzy would clean and Virginia would tag along, but she ended up cleaning more thoroughly than her sisters. It was her nature to pay attention to detail. She was perhaps too scrupulous in this matter. It began to weigh heavily on her a time grew on. Gramma paid very well, but the younger sister did not see any of it until much later when she cleaned by herself for her grandmother.

Virginia would also tag along with her older sisters when they went ot babysit. She would be company for her sisters, but until she babysat on her own would she get recompense. She went with her sister Lizzy up to the lake where Aunt Anne and Uncle John were renting at the time. Easy to blush, Uncle John picked on the child about her mis-matched socks suggesting that she has another pair just like them somewhere.

Another embarrassing moment was when she went up the street with Annie to watch Connie and Cooney Peter's children. Virginia had fallen asleep and she was groggy going out the door. She nearly fell on the ice. Cooney had a great laugh having just come from the K of C and partaking of a few libations. If that was not enough for the girl, earlier in the evening, little Susie hid behind a door and quietly said "Boo" as Virginia went by. Virginia was caught off guard and she let out a war whoop that is still being talked about. On another occasion, Virginia went to babysit with Lizzy at the lake where one of their cousins had a camp. One cousin told Virginia that she was weird - something she never forgot.

Annie would usually buy pop tarts or bananas with her babysitting money. If the family were heading down to Glens Falls, they would stop at the Freighofer outlet and get day old bread and cookies.

Church

St. Mary's is a beautiful, neo-gothic style church literally in the backyard of where Virginia grew up. The school property was owned by the Farleighs and rented for a dollar a year. The church had sustained a couple of fires over the years. It contains the relics of Saint Isaac Jogues in its marble Altar Table.

Virginia loved going to church. The Mass fulfilled her. Besides attending Mass daily during Lent, Virginia was especially hard on herself. She would give up all candy, soda and chips in addition to giving up her favorite sitcom of "Gomer Pyle". Her brother Thomas caught her taping it with a tape recorder in which she planned to listen to it after Lent.

The family was very creative. They would make up plays and put on skits for their parents and the rest of the family. They were great for impersonating local folks - everyone was fair game including aunts and uncles. It was fun to mimic one aunt's Southern accent. There was a lady in town who Lizzy called 'Alfred Hitchcock'. She was originally from Long Island. Virginia would imitate her. Her father liked her impersonations. The brothers got in on it too. They owuld imitate John Wayne as did their father and Uncle Cyrus. There was a lot of laughter and banter in this stucco house where there was four to a bedroom. Moreover, they all looked out for each other.

Nicknames

Daddy had nicknames for all the children. Henry was 'Chester" and sometimes "Que pasa", or "Meat". Henry was on crutches after he fell from a truck when he was in the eighth grade. It was in the early Spring -

Holy Saturday. It was very serious. He was rushed to Burlington. He had a blood clot. he had to have a pin put in his ankle. His mouth was all stitched up. Poor Uncle Tommy - covered in blood. He was driving the truck on Shanahan Road while Henry was holding brush down in the back. That was when the accident happened. Henry limped after that. There was a tv character named 'Chester' who had a limp. There was also a man named 'Chester' who worked at the Roger's Rock Club. He was a chauffeur of African American descent. Grampa used to tell humorous stories behind the scenes where Chester was involved. Karl was called "Kevin Roach". Daddy would sing in this beautiful tenor voice, "My name is Kevin Roach". Lizzy was "Ellsworth". Annie was "Boone" or "Flower". Mary was

"Chooz" because she ws always looking for her shoes and that is how she pronounced it. Virginia was "Little 'v'" or "Pineapple" curiously enough. Aunt Mary said it was because she was hospitable, but it really had more to do with the way Virginia looked in the fifth grade. If she were a fruit, she would have been a pineapple. Virginia was always rolling her eyes and smirking and doing these peculiar expressions. Karlene was "Auto" and her siblings called her "Car Car". Tisdale was "Murphy" or "Mark 5". Thomas was "Sargeant". Sarah was called "Ethel". The nicknames were whatever struck Daddy's fancy. Most of the kids went by their middle names oddly enough. Not sure if Georgie and Jane had nicknames. One day, Daddy would have his own nickname. Karl started it - it was "The Old Man" or "Oldie". It was meant affectionately or just hopping on the bandwagon of the early '70's. Virginia made a wooden key holder inthe shape of a large key engraved with this new nickname.

The "Old Man" was really a handsome man with dark ahir and dark eyes. George was clean-shaven when the children were little, but later adopted the full beard like his father. He was witty and quiet - even shy. He had the finest of everything growing up: good food as his mother was an excellent cook, quality clothing, history books, musical instruments - indeed he had a natural ability to play by ear. He had several dogs too. One of his dogs was named 'Butch'. His grandfather was a state senator and he lived next door. Geroge went to Tabor Academy. One of his classmates was the son of a Greek tycoon. George had a sister who went to Emma Willard in Troy as did her mother before her. Jane Fonda was a classmate and this particular aunt would recall how her famous father would come to visit there. There was a younger brother Cyrus who was really like an older brother to George's children as he was so much younger than he. He was the same age as mother's brother Sherrie who also seemed like an older brother.

Watching the Parade 4th of July

Summer Time

Summers meant swimming up at the lake at Gramma Farleigh's camp on Lake George. There was "The Best Fourth in The North" complete with a parade featuring Canadian bagpipe bands. They were wearing all their regalia. There were the pie eating contests which the kids would enter, and yes, win at the Fireman's Field. There would be the fireman's water hose fight the night before on the main street downtown. The hoses were hooked up to the hydrants in front of the Post Office. There was the Greased Pig contest which Karl pretty near won. The Audettes would sit on their front lawn with flags and Indian headbands on or baseball caps. They would watch the parade. Uncle Tommy was close by taking pictures as he was quite the photography buff. It was fireworks and wearing a white Fort Ticonderoga sweatshirt. Mother would load the kids in the Ford station wagon and bring them up to the hill in front of the hospital to watch the fireworks. Then they would go to their cousins the Kingsleys up at the lake and celebrate with sparklers. The boys wore tricorn hats. Mom would take the children to pick strawberries at Densemore's Farm. Then they would stop at Price's Farm to get fresh corn. Corn and strawberry shortcake was the meal du jour in the summer at the Audette household. There was watermelon too.

Virginia was in her first parade when she was eight years old. She was wearing her Brownie uniform carrying the American Flag marching down Weedville Hill. This was a Memorial Day Parade. The parade ended right across from the big house on the Central School lawn. The Brass Band from the Ticonderoga High school was playing there near the monument dedicated to the World War I soldiers. The Band in later years played next to the American Legion on Main Street or "Exchange Street" as it used to be known

Little sister's birthday fell in the summer. Gramma Audette would take her down to Cook & Sacco's and buy her a new striped shirt, blue shorts and Buster Brown sneakers.

Mother was great for making it fun and taking the children out for treats. She would take them out for soft ice cream either at the "Double M" on the Fort Road, or to Thatcher's on the Hague Road. The Milton neighbors

To Virginia, custard was a smooth vanilla sauce like pudding. Virginia always got the chocolate and vanilla swirl ice cream. She urged her brother Thomas to try it, but he only would get the straight chocolate. One time, one of the school teachers came over to make a fuss over the children. He was Mr. Bush but he had a nickname of "Tuffy or Toughy" Bush. he was a very pleasant fellow. Of course the children were all full of giggles. His wife was wonderful - Elsie Bush. She taught little Virginia in the fifth grade at St. Mary's. She was probably Virginia's all-time favorite teacher. She was a kind teacher with pretty blue eyes and always so prettily put together.

In the fifth grade during a recess Valentine's day party, could be heard the then popular song "Itsy Witsy Teen tiny Polka Dot Bikini" with Henry and his "crew" sending paper plates flying like frisbees and narrowly missing Mrs. Bush's head.

One time there was a car accident going up the Portage across from the Audette house. There was broken glass in the road and thankfully the accident was not that bad. Mr. Milton came out of his house and he was helping sweep up the glass. It seems he slipped and thus, earned the nickname "Slippery" by Mr. Audette.

Thomas and Virginia did a lot together growing up. They would walk up to Alexandria Avenue and jump off that bridge where the Lake George begins. They would go swimming there. Their grandfather used to go swimming there too when he was young. Only he mentioned that back then that "turds would float past them!"

Thomas and Virginia would walk on this same road to go to Summer School when Virginia was in fifth grade going into sixth with Thomas a year behind her. The "New School" it was called. It was the first one level, at ground, school in New York State. It had a round design where the kindergarten classrooms were. Virginia's aunt was a kindergarten teacher there for many years. Virginia needed help with her reading when she was about ten years old. The teacher, Mrs. LaTour, would reward candy bars for every ten books read. Little Virginia was rather devious in this effort. She resented that she had to go to summer school in the first place coupled with the possibility that she was a poor reader. She would take out all these books and pretend that she had read them. It was to grate her conscience as time went on and she has since tried to atone for this misdeed.

On their walk home, Thomas and Virginia overheard a woman say, "Are you ready Freddy?" The voice came from a single-wide trailer near the cemetery. From thence, and especially when they came near that place, they would say to each other, "Are you ready Freddy?"

Usually, Annie and Virginia would walk down to the Saveway and get the groceries for supper. Lizzy usually did the cooking though Mother did the meal planning. Sometimes, Mother would drive to the A & P. This real nice man worked there - Mr. Tennian. He had a son who was Georgie's age. Tragically, his son died young. Mr. Tennian also had a daughter Kathy. Lizzy and Kathy were good friends. Mr. Tennian used ot pick on Lizzy when she would pick out yogurt at the A & P. That was when yogurt first came out and it was touted as a weight loss regime. One day, going home from the A & P, on their way down Weedville Hill, Thomas fell out of the back of the station wagon. Virginia said, "Mommy, Thomas fell out of the car." Mother exclaimed, "Oh my Godfrey! Where is he?!" "He is back there in the road." Poor Mom. This may have been when Thomas had to go to the hospital in Burlington. Mother would often say, "Oh my Godfrey!" When asked why, she said there was this man in TV Land named Arthur Godfrey. Gramma Farleigh used to say it too. They did not swear.

Mother

Virginia was named for her mother, the oldet girl born to Gramma and Gransieur Farleigh.

Mother had that MGM star quality about her. She has bright hazel eyes and a scintillating smile that lights up a room. She also had a zest for learning. She would don a dab of lipstick and the glamor shone through.

On special occasions, she would wear Chanel No. 5. Moreover, she was kind, and soft and considerate to everyone. She was brains, beauty and compassion all in one. This Virginia was a wordsmith. She attended Saint Rose College in Albany and completed her Library of Science degree. She did this at a time when it was uncommon - driving two hundred miles after having taught all day to attend night classes - and this, sometimes in terrible snowstorms. Little Virginia remembers being mesmerized by the snow falling against the windshield of the car on those long rides. Karl used to accompany his mother most times. He was very clever and he would find things to do to entertain himself at the University while his mother attended the night classes. One of the things he did, was take his St. Mary's school photo and affix it to a dollar bill and run it through a xerox machine. He would come home with these fresh minted bills. His brothers and sisters thought they were so cool. He also would do origami and teach his younger siblings how to make three dimensional birds and such out of a single piece of paper. Karl aslo devised his own radio station which he conducted from his bedroom. he wired it in such a way tht the kids could hear it in the kitchen. He would start by playing Cat Stevens "Morning Has Broken" and then the sound effects to eggs being whisked against a bowl could be ehard as scrambled eggs were the featured breakfast item.

The kids were all fascinated when Mother would get her hair done. She would come home with a new perm. All the children would lightly pat her head. Henry said it felt like a brillo pad. Virginia used to like to comb her brothers' hair. She especially liked to run her hands over their fresh crew cuts. She would comb her father's hair too.

Mother might have gotten her hair done to attend a teachers conference/retreat at Grossingers. It was somewhere in the Catskills. The kids would miss their mother terribly. She never uttered a harsh word. When she returned home, she would present each of the children with a chocolate lollipop. Only these were different. There would be white chocolate on one side with a picture of maybe an airplane or an automobile and milk chocolate on the other side.

Mother had these large jadeite colored Rosary beads that hung on the bedpost. They would glow in the dark when the lights were off. Every night she would say to each and everyone of her children, "Good Night, God Bless you and I love you." Only, it sounded like, "Good Night, God Bless you nigh love you."

Faith of Our Fathers

Mom was a devout Catholi with a devout Catholic mother and an episcopalian father. Daddy had a very Catholic father and an Episcopalian mother. Grampa said that Gramma Audette was a "High Episcopalian" as she would pray the rosary. Grampa Audette had ordered her a pre-dieu as she was very prayerful.

Daddy had served in the Air Force during the Korean War. He and Mom lived in Maryland when they were first married. Then they returned to Ticonderoga to raise theri family. Daddy worked with Grampa at the Fort running the soda fountain and the concessions. Mom taught Latin and gym class in Mineville. Little Virginia would note how her mother would take a Hershey bar from the econd dreser drawer, hidden from the kids, and she would put it in her purse to take to school. Later, she would ask her mother what she was doing with all those candy bars. Her mother had told her about a handicapped boy who she would see. She would give him the candy bars when she saw him. This always stuck with the younger Virginia. Her mother set a good example from the start.

Cigarette smoking was common when little Virginia was growing up. The Servicemen were given cigarettes in the Armed Forces. Drinking seemed to be common too. People in town had bridge parties and cocktail hours. Only Daddy was affected by this so-called norm. It was more serious than a fondness for the drink as it rendered him physically ill. It was dehabilitating. His own father could hold his own, but alcohol had an adverse effect on his sons. One day, Daddy could not get out of bed. He would black out and be lying sideways on the bed. Grampa would come down and talk to him sternly. It was of no avail. The children would make egg nogs and steak tartar to revive him. This very complex and humorous man was trapped. It was thus. Grampa got into plumbing and had his son apprentice with him as a father can make allowances. The children were very protective of their father. No one would come in the house.

It must have been difficult for Mother but she did what she had to do. She loved George. She also had the makings of a saint. She worked tirelessly. When she was not working, she was giving birth and nurturing her twelve children. She never complained. The older brothers were very helpful when Daddy was indisposed. Naturally her own family would want the best for her. Some things are hard to comprehend but it is a strange thing about love - it does conquer all, if not sooner then later.

Sundays

Mother and Father would join the Audette grandparents for Sunday dinner. Maud Leach taught Gramma Audette how to cook. one of her signature dishes was a rack of lamb infused with garlic and served with mint jelly. Maud was the family maid. She was also an old maid living to the age of 104. She was an excellent seamstress too. She made these beautiful aprons by hand for Grandmother. She would give her one every Christmas. Maud used to take care of Uncle Cyrus when he was a baby. She loved bing cherries. Grandfather would get her some in June when they were in season.

While their parents were having Sunday dinner, the girls would let lose in the house blasting records of Carole King, Sonny & Cher, Carly Simon or Burt Bacharach. They would dance and sing holding their hairbrushes as microphones. They had a lot of imagination.

Grampa's mother and father were good cooks too. They were in the restuarant business. They ran 'The Palm Restaurant' which is where Newberry's five and dime store was later. "They ran the Rex" restuarant before that which was named for Grampa's dog. Rex was smarter than a whip. Newberry's five and dime came in there later. Grampa used to polish the brass spittons there. Those were the days of individual shops. There was Gallant's shoe store, Petty's Barber Shop, there was a millinery shop at the foot of Champlain Avenue next to a beauty parlor. Exchange Street is where all commercial activity took place. The Audette's would get their gas at Towne's Garage. It was an Esso Gas Station with a bright orange and black tiger for its mascot.

A Trip to the City

When Virginia was going on twelve years old, she and her two older sisters visited New York City. It was during Easter vacation. Little Virginia went next door to the big house to wash her yellow raincoat for the trip. When Gramma saw it, and this after it had come out of the dryer, she said, "Aren't you going to wash it?!" She had already done so and she was too embarrassed to admit that to her grandmother. Next thing, Annie and Virginia were getting bright new yellow raincoats from Cooke & Sacco. Lizzy already had a beautiful turquoise colored one that used to be cousin Mary Pat's.

Uncle H.G. drove his nieces to Albany. It was a quiet ride except for the girlish giggles along the way. Uncle Tommy met them and drove them the rest of the way to Tarrytown which is just North of the city. He and Aunt Arthurlyn had an apartment there.

This was a trip to remember. When they got in, their uncle ordered take-out pizza which was a first for them. The girls were silly laughing at everything and nothing; most likely there was a passing of gas incident. Mother taught the children to refer to these "sounds" as "poopanoises". "Traf" was more tolerant than that other crude word. They woke up to one of Uncle Tommy's favorites, Petula Clark's "I Never Promised You a Rose Garden" which is kind of funny if indeed there was flatulence.

Uncle Tommy and Aunt Arthurlyn took the girls on a tour. First, it was to the Lynhurst Mansion where a favorite tv show was filmed. Then, it was to the Empire State Building. They got to pick out a souvenir at the top. Virginia got a pen that had a bunch of different colors - the kind that you could push down whatever desired color you wanted. It had a picture of The Empire State Building on it. Virginia could not decide between that, or the bronze miniature of the famous landmark. Then it was on to Radio City Music Hall. They saw the Rockettes there. Uncle Tommy commented on how glad he was that the girls had those bright colored raincoats on as they were easy to keep track of.

Aunt Arthurlyn is a terrific cook. She comes from Georgia. She cooked a delicious Southern style meal of fried chicken. Later that night Virginia was thinking that she should have selected that replica statue of The Empire State Building. She was overheard talking to her sisters. Her uncle asked her why she did not get the other one. Sunday they went to Saint Patrick's Cathedral to Mass. Afterward, they went to a park on the Hudson River where Uncle Tommy put coins in the view finder so the girls could get a close-up view of The Statue of Liberty. This was Virginia's first trip to "The Big Apple", but it would not be her last.

One of little Virginia's favorite gifts that she received for Christmas is pink elephant piggy bank. Aunt Arthurlyn and Uncle Tommy gave her this. It had big white fuzzy ears with polka dots on the inside. It was made of a hard plastic and it smelled like the new dolls that the girls also got at Christmas.

She also got a new pair of ice skates. She and her brothers and sisters would head over to the skating rink on Schuyler Street and go ice skating. There was a shed where the youngsters could go in to get warm. The feet always seem to get cold. Sometimes, there would be a special day there and they would have hot dogs and hot chocolate.

On another occasion, Virginia received a candle making kit. This proved problematic - even for a plumber. The young girl poured the liquid parafin down the sink drain and it molded into the shape of the pipe beneath.

Virginia enjoyed crafts. She would spend her pocket money on "loopers" to make potholders and other crafts that she would pick up at the hardware store.

Other Holidays

The Audette children would dye over four dozen eggs on Holy Saturday and each would put at least three eggs in his or her basket. The Easter Bunny hid the baskets after filling them with new socks and handkerchieves which would be worn along with a new Easter bonnet at the Easter Sunday Mass. The Easter Bunny always brought the good chocolate from Meyer's Drugstore. Ham dinner was savored after Mass.

The day before Thanksgiving, Mother would purchase a new sheet from J.J. Newberry's. It would serve as a tablecloth in the dining room, but later,it would be relegated for one of the beds. In the center of the table would be a large bowl of fruit. There would be apples, oranges, grapes, bananas and pears. Candles were lit, and favors were set at each place. These dixie cups contained peanuts, raisins, pastel mints and chocolate M & M's. There were two kinds of cranberry - the jellied and the whole berry. Pickles and olives were set out in crystal dishes with little silver forks. Fresh cider was poured, and turkey with stuffing was served complete with acorn squash filled with pure maple syrup and real butter, peas, mashed potatoes and gravy, creamed onions and turnip. Then Little Virginia would do the dishes as she generally did. She usually washed the dishes three times a day. Her brother Karl called her "Cinderella". After the clean-up, Mother would whip fresh cream and the family would continue the feast with Lizzy's homemade apple and pumpkin pies. There was also a mince pie on hand. Annie would then chase Henry around the house with a pin in her hand threatening to "pop" him!

Stone School

The youngsters would play "Stone School" on the front steps of their home. Bushes of 'Bridal Veil' grew in front of the porch. The porch was a great gathering place growing up. Life could be viewed from here. Mother used to tell the children not to sit on stone as they might get a kidney infection. They were also told not to wear their rubber galoshes in the house as it was bad for their eyes. There were two stumps in front of the house. Virginia used to leap in the air and flutter from one stump to the other. She imagined that she could fly in all those striped shirts! The little sidewalk leading up to the porch swirled like "The Yellow Brick Road" in 'The Wizard of Oz'. The kids would play hopscotch there and avoid stepping on the cracks. They would catch fireflies when it got dark in the summer. They would rake up piles of leaves to jump in come the Fall. They would play whiffle ball in the side yard between their house and the big house. They would play "Hide and Seek" with the neighbors and shouts of "Ollie, Ollie income free!" The neighbors across the street were a beautiful family. Daddy always commented on the beauty of the Mrs. Hanson. The children inherited her beauty besides being nice.

They would watch the daily meanderings of the local characters going up and down the street. There was one lady who walked up and down the historical Portage. Her name was Joyce Crammond. She would go to the store to get her groceries. One day, she had a new cart with wheels on it. The children were happy to see this. Grampa used to call her "Step and Fetch It". Father O'Reilly said that she was beautiful in her own unique way. She had a beautiful smile and her eyes would light up. She was very bright though she did things in a methodical if slow fashion. She was neatly groomed coming from humble means. She had a sister who was housebound. She may have been in a wheelchair. I never saw her, but Grampa tole me about her. Sadly, she died young. Joyce did wear a little red lipstick. This stood out against her pale complexion. She was tall and lanky and most likely did not get all her daily nutritional requirements. She spoke eloquently. She was highly intelligent and a Faithful communicant at St. Mary's. In later years, Mrs. Dechame took her under her wing. Irene Hall also looked out for her. One time, Virginia came home to find some items that Joyce had left for her. Joyce had given her late sister's little gold cross necklace to Virginia. She had also given her a gold and amethyst ring. Virginia was very touched by this. Joyce had told her that the tiny crosses were what they wore back then.

Going up Champlain Avenue, which runs parallel to the Portage, was another character. He was pale too. Oddly enough, his surname was "Blood". He looked like a ghost from Fort Ticonderoga. He too was highly intelligent. He knew his history. he wore a black beret with the traditional Scottish red and black dicing around the crown. Little festoons adorned it. He had an unusual walking stick. He had black hair and eyes that matched. This was no other than Eprhraim Blood. He used to stop and talk to me. Something about his voice made me think that his lungs must have been congested. Indeed he did smoke the pipe. I believe that he took care of his mother and then he lived alone after she died. He must have been lonely. It is said that he had an enormous comic book collection. Oh, to have that collection today! I used to go snowshoeing up on Mount Defiance in the winter. I liked to go at night time to gaze at the stars. Later, I learned that Mr. Blood used to up there in the night though I never had that eerie encounter.

Speaking of Mount Defiance, another eerie thought, are those big black snakes that go up in the trees there. One time, when Grampa was working at the Fort, he went to move what he thought was a big, black rubber hose, - only, 'lo and behold, it was not a hose, but the former!

The Lady in the Library

One thing that Little Virginia loved about school was going to the library. A very dear lady volunteered there. She was, Stephanie Sarah Pell Dechame - Mrs. Dechame. She was the most fascinating lady. She grew up with a silver spoon attending a French boarding school in Switzerland. However, she was a modest and gracious lady. She was tenderhearted towards the less fortunate. She also had a great love for animals. This was widely known and some people took advantage of that. They would drop off their cats or dogs at her house knowing she could not turn them away. She was also gifted with a prescience - sensing things before they happened. She dreamt about the German soldiers ransacking her grandmother's chateau shortly before it actually happened. She had a sort of Doris Day charm about her. Mrs. Dechame dressed beautifully too. She would give little gifts to Virginia. Thus began a lifelong correspondence. Often they were writing thank you notes for thank you notes. Virginia also helped arrange books in the library with Mrs. Dechame. Mrs. Dechame's grandfather was responsible for the restoration of Fort Ticonderoga.

The Post Office

The child had a fascination with the Post Office. She loved writing letters.
She had pen pals, and she was always sending away for things on the back
of cereal boxes or in the back of a comic book. Once, she got a 'Pan Am'
airplane model in the mail. Another time there was a "Jolly Green Giant"
made out of vinyl. She gave this one to her dear friend Christine. She
ordered a bright yellow T-shirt with her name on it from "Cheerios". She
always believed what the description of the item was with all its
embellishments. She took it literally and that was not always the case.
One time, she went next door to the big house to ask Gramma Farleigh for
three paper bags as she needed three bags to send to the Planter's
Peanut Company. They were double brown paper bags, very sturdy.
Virginia sent them out and a week later she received not one, but three
coloring books fo the U.S. Presidents. The folks at the Planter's Company
must have gotten an awful kick out of this because it was supposed to
have been three peanut bags which were small and the peanuts may have
cost ten cents a bag. Daddy would go and pick up the mail. Virginia was
always excited when the mail came.

No one had anything against the child, but it pained her that she was
always the last one picked to be on a team. She would dream about being
picked as captain and then picking the last ones to be first. That
opportunity never came.

Virginia did love Saint Mary's and her classmates. She felt very close to
them and she continues to feel that bond today.   She was very touched
when her brother Henry told her that the class was praying for her wehn
she had to be taken down to Dr. Tom's office because her forearm looked
"bumpy" after a TB shot. A boy in the third grade had to go too.
Thankfully both students were alright.

Virginia did have her share of sore throats though. She was afflicted with
severe hay fever when she was thirteen. The worse pain that stands out
is an ear ache (infection) that she had when she was not quite ten years
old. The pain was excruciating. There was a Jerry Lewis movie on TV but

that could not even distract the girl. She probably played it down to her parents. On another occasion, thre was a mirror with a sharp edge that fell on her ankle. The child should have had a Tetnus shot and stitches, but she was too afraid to tell anyone. She has a deep scar as a result.

The Four Little Girls

Karlene takes great pride in reminding everyone how Virginia got the four "little girls" washed and dressed for school in the morning. Mother ordered the sweetest little cotton frocks from Best & Company for the girls. Virginia would lay these out the night before. Virginia would take the girls next door to the big house and use the downstairs full bathroom to ready her sisters. Jane, a sweet, generous child was in Kindergarten and Mary was in First Grade. Karlene and Tisdale went to Mrs. Bileaux's for Nursery School. Later,Mrs. Bileaux would teach Virginia how to sew when she was in the 4-H Club.

After school, Virginia would devise games to play with the four little girls. She made up a little club for them. The whole family would play various board games. Karl was unbeatable at Monopoly. The kids would paly "croquet" outdoors in the summer. Uncle Tommy gave the family a croquet set one year, and a badminton set another year.

Sixth Grade

Sister John Matha was Virginia's homeroom teacher in the sixth grade. She was a frail nun with a white face and large light brown eyes. She was delicate but fervent in the Faith. She asked if anyone could recite 'The Apostle's Creed' during religion class. Virginia could have, but she was too shy to speak up and she did not want to be the only one. Anyway, she seemed to have a soft spot for the Audette girl. She had asked her to come to the convent after school. She had a pair of black rubber zip-up boots that came mid-calf and had fur trim. She wanted Virginia to have these. She also gave her a black "nuns" coat. It was a lovely coat but the thought of wearing it was too much for little Virginia. It was from one of the fine shops in Watertown.

The students switched classrooms in junior high. Mrs. McKeown taught English. She is unsurpassed - the best and most thorough English teacher ever. She was sought after by other schools, but her heart was with St. Mary's. She was very attractive too as were all her sisters. Her blonde hair was swept up in a French twist. She wore high heels too. Her little brother was in Virginia's class. She got a kick out of Henry and Tony B. also known as "Bones". There was "Cockroach" too. Tony would walk by and expel gas. Mrs. McKeown would try hard not to laugh. She would say, "Alright 'Windy', get back in the classroom."

There was one girl in the 7th grade that Virginia liked very much. Her name was Michelle. She used to bring her in cinnamon buns for her family. Grampa used to buy day-old buns from the Grand Union. He would get a huge box of bread and baked goods for the Audette family. Michelle invited Virginia to her house. Michelle's mother made the creamiest macaroni and cheese. Michelle's sister wshed Virginia's hair in the kitchen sink. She used Palmolive dish detergent. Michelle showed Virginia a picture of her brother. No one knew where he was. He was in Vietnam - that is all they knew. Then one day, Michelle came to school very sad. Her younger brother Eddie died. Eddie was a sweet and happy boy. It was a self-inflicted. Then Michelle started to ask Virginia about Evolution. It seems the Jehovah's Witnesses appealed to her family during their bereavement. Michelle's father was such a sweet, kind gentleman. Eddie was like his father. It was very sad.

One of the mothers in the parish gave Virginia's mother some 'hand-me-downs'. There was a pair of suede shoes with light blue in the middle of them styled like a saddle. They were square-toed. They fit Virginia perfectly even though they looked very much like a pair that her classmate wore last year. Sure enough, her classmate recognized them, "Hey, I used to have a pair of shoes identical to them." This confirmed what Virginia suspected but the former owner was a nice girl. She never brought it up again. Her mother probably never told her that she gave them away.

Virginia made her Confirmation in the 7th grade. Bishop Brzanna came down from Ogdensburgh. Gramma Farleigh was Virginia's sponsor. Virginia took the name "Mary' for her Confirmation name - in honor of Our Blessed Mother. Her mother suggested that name. She is glad she took it as others were taking popular names over Saints' names.

Eighth Grade

Virginia was sort of a pet for Sister Joan Harkness. Virginia used to run errands for her. She would be given penny rolls and go to the Post Office to mail something. It used to try the postal clerk's patience. Then Virginia would bump into this lady who lived on Amherst Avenue. Her name was Margaret Townsend. She could be likened to Emily Dickinson. She was witty. She had blue eyes and a pageboy hairstyle. She would wear blue sneakers and a London Fog raincoat. She used to comment on Virginia's hair. She admired it. Margaret never married. She took care of her mother. She lived in one of the old Mill houses. If you were to go in, it was like stepping into the 1950's - a real time warp. Miss Townsend had taught school in Schroon Lake. She enjoyed seeing all the Audette children sitting on the black wrought iron bar in front of Walsh's house. One thing about Miss Townsend was that she spoke of things that occurred a long time ago, but it was as though it was only yesterday. She would ask Virginia to come to her house to shampoo her mother's hair. Virginia would anticipate going the next day or two, but it would not be for another two weeks or more! Anyway, back to Sister Joan - some of the kids called her Sister Joan "Heartless". This made Virginia feel bad. Sister Joan liked to talk to Virginia. She treated her as a friend more than a student. Consequently, she would put little gifts in her symposium project for the teacher. It might be a Bic pen or a chocolate bar. One time she included an article by Betty Friedan in her project. Her father had done plumbing at her summer camp. Her writing would not have been what Sister Joan was looking for at Catholic Junior High. Virginia was hopelessly naive. Sister Joan told the class that extra points would be given if the students asked their classmates questions after their presentations. Poor Mark Karkoski - "What exactly is the Reproduction

System?" came the query from the young girl. The room went quiet with a lot of red faces. Then Sister Joan closed it up with some genral statement that still left the girl in a quandary.

It was Holy Saturday when Virginia's brother Henry was seriously injured. Henry was holding down brush on the back of a truck heading to the dump with Uncle Tommy. Henry fell off. He was rushed to Burlington. Uncle Tommy was distraught and covered in blood. Henry had a blood clot and he had emergency surgery with a pin being put in his ankle. His mouth was cut up bad too. Everyone prayed for him at church that evening. He had just had his foot washed during the Holy Thursday Service. He had his left foot washed and it was unmarred. His right foot and leg took the blow. He had a big cast. He was in the hospital for a good week before coming home. When he first got home, Henry stayed at the big house. There were many visitors. One, was a little neighbor boy who lived across the street - Tommy Hanson. He looked so forlorn sitting on the sofa, but he just wanted to be with Henry to offer some sort of comfort. He was several years younger. It was such a sweet gesture.

Eighth grade graduation came and both Henry and Virginia received awards for "Outstanding" Boy and Girl. This meant a lot to Virginia. Henry received the Spelling award too and Virginia was pleased to receive the English award as she loved English.

Virginia felt bad that Henry was unable to make the 8th grade class trip. It was to Montreal to Saint Joseph's Oratory and to the great Exposition site of 1967 "Man and His World". Virginia slept downstairs the night before on a cot in the dining room. Mother gave her twenty dollars and she woke to the church bells. She ran over to the school lot to get on the bus. Virginia went on the Ferris Wheel and the roller coaster. She was most in awe by the splendor of Notre Dame Basilica.

Besides babysitting, Virginia's first official job on paper was picking strawberries at Densemore's Farm on the Hague Road. This is when she was afflicted with severe hayfever. Her nose would not stop running and her eyes swelled. It was not in her to quit though her Aunt Mary was concerned for her. Her aunt also use to say that Virginia would give a religious vocation to the family. While it was a nice compliment, it also may have put an expectation on her.

High School

The painfully shy girl came out of her shell when she entered high school. She really blossomed and threw herself into every extra-curricular activity. The lady who worked alongside the nurse in her office wrote in her year book not to get burned out as she was surely burning the candle at both ends. She kept going though. She was in Drama Club, Latin Club, Drill Team, Field Hockey, Track, French Club, and Key Club. She was in so many different things that if you were to look in the year book, you would see no less than forty diffent things that she belonged to in the course of her high school years.

The first few days of high school marked a sad passage. One of the new teacher's, who was taking attendance, would call out a girl's name. However, she was in the Burlington Hospital dying. Every breath was a struggle. She did not make it through the first week. Virginia was deeply affected by this. She remembered going to her younger sister's wake when she was in the second grade. Kim had made it this far having suffered with the same lung disease. Her name was still being called out. It was a very sad time. Virginia went to the wake with Cynthia Bileaux. They had just come from Drill Team practice so they were wearing their Drill Team uniforms. Virginia bent over to remove the bells from her sneakers. She was so overcome that she dard not go straight home. She stood outside the tower window next door the big house weeping copiously. Kim had started at St. Mary's and then had gone to the "new school" so she did not know her well. However, her death affected her deeply. She would visit Kim' parents throughout high school. She also collected funds for Cystic Fibrosis.

There was another tragic incident in her freshman year. One of the fellows, who was helping direct a play that Virginia was in, took his life. The play was canceled. Virginia sang in the folk choir at the funeral.

Theater

At this stage in her life, Virginia thought that she would like to be an actress. She and Kelly Croton would stay after school while Mis Salerno would coach them on fine acting. After school, Virginia would go down the street to tutor a young neighbor in Math. In return, the neighbor's mother would allow Virginia to take dance classes for free. The dance instructor was a former Rockette. Virginia had seen the Rockettes when she went to the city with Uncle Tommy and Aunt Arthurlyn. Betty Wilson was married to the author Sloan Wilson. She taught Ballet. The only other dance instruction that Virginia had was when she was in the third grade. She went with her two older sisters Annie and Lizzy to Norma Strong's to learn 'Tap'. She was always out of step and very self-conscious. She also went over to that same street, two houses up, to accompany her same sisters as they took piano lessons. It was like watching paint dry for the young girl. There was a music meter on top of the piano while attempts at "Turkey in The Straw" were being made. Virginia sat quietly in the corner in a rocking chair watching the meter swing next to the box of Russell Stover chocolates. She was bored out of her mind, but she sat patiently. Lizzy actually had quite a gift with the piano. She could play by ear.

Strange Friends

Virginia's brother Karl suggested that she take typing as it would come in very handy. One day, she received a type-written letter in the mail. It threatened her and her mother. Virginia had an idea of the sender. In fact, there was a corner stamp on the envelope just like the one that was missing on the sheet of stamps at this person's house. Virginia confronted this girl and she told her how the police might get involved and that her mother was upset. Virginia exaggerated this and the girl admitted to it. She was always putting Virginia down. She could not believe that Virginia was a cousin to her sister's friend who was popular. She bullied Virginia and Virginia was uncomfortable in her presence as this person would go out of her way to embarrass Virginia. Virginia tried to overlook these things and she came to understand that was the way she was. Perhaps she could not help it. The girl did have some conscience as in her guilt, she took a bottle of her mother's perfume to give to Virginia's mother for reparation. That same bottle found its way in Virginia's Christmas stocking. Yes, VIrginia, there is a Santa Claus!

Betty Wilson's dance studio opened up a whole new world to the teenager. She would go down to the studio and put records on and dance her heart out when no one was there. Then one day Betty's father came over from Ireland. He added onto the studio building an apartment for himself. It was like a loft painted in bright colors. It reminded Virginia of something that you would see in the Yankee magazine. His name was Robert Stevens. He thought Virginia put color on her eyelids. He could not believe that they were naturally the color that they were. She had big blue eyes which reminded her father of Goldie Hawn. Mr. Stevens told the girl how he ate cat food one time for dinner by accident. His wife did not want to worry him when she discovered it as she loved him very much.

Virginia met Lynn clarke at the dance studio. She was a lot of fun. She was even protective of Virginia. She had invited her new friend to her house for a pajama party. Lynn had a pretty green turtle neck shirt. She wanted Virginia to have it, but she did not want to insult her. So she put it up for grabs. Another girl from the Baldwin Road took it, but it was a sweet gesture on Lynn's part.

Lynn and Virginia got to go to New York City with the Wilsons and take a dance class with local legned Daniel Leavitt. His mentor, was the father of actor Richard Thomas (The Walton's). Virginia and Lynn would traipse around the city stopping at Tiffany's. They would purchase something from the Clearance section and pretend to be living high off the hog. Long before selfies and digital cameras came on the scene, they would take pictures with their bulky cameras at the various landmarks - pretending to be movie stars.

One day, Lynn told Virginia that her neighbor Mrs. Belden was having a garage sale. She was selling her silver fox jacket for twenty-five bucks. Virginia got right on this. She came home wearing the new fur. And to Mrs. Belden's horror, Virginia was wearing it to school and storing it in her locker!

In-between Lynn's family's house and the Belden house is a garage. A very sad circumstance took place there. The former owners of Lynn's house died in their car garage. There is speculation that they fell on hard times. They ran a hotel. When Lynn was little, she often saw a lady when she was in her room. The lady seemed to look out for her.

Virginia spent a lot of time at Lynn's house in High School. Lynn's mother was a great cook. She would make Lynn the most delicous maple walnut cake with lots of layers in it for her birthday. She also made these jam strip cheeser things. Virginia and Lynn would go out on the upstairs deck and sunbathe. They would also go out on the paddle boat or the "sun fish" sail boat.

Virginia also babysat for Betty's daughter Jelissa. Jelissa was a very unusual child. She had every exotic animal under the sun. She wanted to become a veterinarian. Often Virginia had to clean out her pet cages. Jelissa also had a pet skunk named 'Lilac'. One day, Lilac got loose. Jelissa was very upset. Virginia spotted a skunk over in St. Mary's playground.

She thought surely this was the same skunk that Jelissa lost. She went over and very gingerly, followed the skunk. She tried to retrieve it but it scooted under the rectory as she was trying to grab it. Suffice is to say, Virginia got doused good! She smelled like a skunk for at least a month. It didn't matter how many showers she took or how much tomato juice she used. Sloan Wilson did commend her for her efforts though. One man in town, Basil Donovan, called Virginia "Skunky" from then on. He even made her a decoupage of a skunk on wood for Christmas.

Virginia also was a companion for Jelissa's paternal grandmother - Ruth Wilson. Old Mrs. Wilson was a graduate of Vassar. She was always encouraging Virginia to go there. She would use the chairlift to go upstairs. Her granddaughter used to taunt her by using the remote control sending the old lady up an down the stairs mercilessly.

Then one day Annie told her sister that Mr. Stevens died. She felt sorry for his daughter Betty. She went down to the Saveway store and picked up some Freighofer eclairs. Whe presented them to Mr. Wilson as he answered the door to their house on Champlain Avenue.

Growing Pains

One troublesome incident occurred when Virginia went on a ski trip to Gore Mountain. She was a freshman and her sister Lizzy let her borrow her new skis that she got for Christmas. Virginia had never skiied before, but she was open to everything. She came home that Saturday evening with broken skis or at least one fiber glass ski broken in half. It was remarkable that she was unscathed - physically anyway. Everyone was at the Vigil Mass. Virginia was full of dread taking to her bed hoping and praying that it would all go away. She heard Henry downstairs laughing and making jokes about the ski. How would Lizzy take it. Her father went up to her and he consoled her. Virginia vowed that she would give Lizzy her babysitting money for the rest of her life.

Candystriper

Virginia became a candystriper when she turned 13. She wore the red and white striped jumper with a white blouse underneath and a little cap on her head. She enjoyed this very much. Lynn was one too. They would get into some awful antics at the old Moses Ludington Hospital. One patient from Port Henry, an elderly woman named Wilma whenever asked anything, would reply in this long, drawn out voice, "Well, I don't know," or "Well, I don't care." One time, Wilma insisted that Virginia wear this big bow on her head. Virginia complied. Then, everytime when it was time for the food to come up on the elevator, instead, Dr. Hoffner would be getting off the elevator. They would laugh. So the two decided to refer to this doctor as "the food". The "food" rather resembled Einstein. Virginia would also ride on the carts. Lynn would push her. One time she inadvertently gave a diabetic a piece of candy; another time a patient scheduled for surgery asked the girl for water. She was compassionate despite her mis-guided intentions. Her brother would never let her live that down either.

Lynn understood Virginia. They shared a great sense of humor. There was this man in town named 'Edmund Frechette' or 'Undie' for short, Hence, the Audettes referred to their undergarments as "Frechettes". Lynn appreciated all the puns and terminology that the Audettes used. Another man in town wore these cranberry colored trousers all the time. His name was Mr. Wallace. "Please pass the 'Mr. Wallace' could be heard at the Audette Thanksgiving table.

Lynn and Virginia would make up names for people using their initials. Lynn was "Lincoln Continental". Fred G. became "Ford Granada"; Gary M. was "General Motors" and Paul G. was "Parental Guidance".

Sometimes Virginia would stay with old Mrs. Wilson at their summer camp known as "The Rookery". This was at the very end of Baldwin Road and in clear sight of Roger's Slide. Mrs. Wilson loved the lake and she was a good swimmer. One early Spring day, she hired a taxi and returned to her haunt. She chose to go for a swim. She succumbed. God rest her.

Her little golden colored house on the top of a hill on Algonkin Street was rented out. One day Virginia was cutting through as she often did, when the tenant stopped her. He worked at the mill, a man in his early 30's. He was also a volunteer fireman. He asked if she could run an errand for him. She complied. He asked her to purchase some nyon panty hose - "No Nonsens" no less and no kidding! She awkwardly delivered them, when the fellow asked her to wait a minute. He changed and put them on with his athletic shorts over them. He wanted to model them for the teenager. Virginia mentioned this to the landlord who brought it to Mr. Wilson's attention. He wrote to a highly acclaimed psychiatrist who wrote back saying that he was likely harmless though he did have a fetish. She took a different way down to the Saveway after that.

Time of Wonder

Henry and some of the boys in high school used to pick on other students if they were an easy mark or have some sort of a foible. One girl, Cheryl Terrell used to slur her 'S's'. Henry, Tony and Cockroach would ask if anyone had seen "S-S- Seryle Terrell". Then poor Kelly Grady had a sticker applied unknowingly to the back of her blouse with letters arranged into a naughty word. Boys wil be ....

One day, Virginia asked her mother if a person could have a baby on her own. Her mother simply said, "It takes two." When her sisters told her the facts of life, she was shocked and even more shocked to think that her neighbors had done so to bear their children. She would never forget the time when Davey McCoy said to her mother at the Saveway store, "What goodies have you got today Mrs. Audette?" as a feminine product was placed on the conveyor belt.

Mrs. Audette was a Latin and French scholar. She looked forward to doing the New York Times Crossword puzzle every Sunday - in ink!

Virginia wore skirts or dresses almost every day to school. Once in a while she would don her overalls and a striped shirt. She also made good use of the gym shower at school as it was accessible compared to getting in the bathroom at home.

In high school Virginia was viewed as everyone's sister. Mickey Patrick would call her up and talk at length about his travails. A boy in homeroom might tap her on her shoulder, but Virginia was oblivious. She was so engrossed in all the extra-curricular activities. Oh there was one fellow, a year ahead of her, and he could imitate Groucho Marx. He was thoroughly charming but once Mary O'Reilly decided to tell him that Virginia had a crush on him, forget it. There was a lot of talent at Ti High. Besides Larry with his impersonations, Eddie Stanilka was the master. He rivaled RIch Little's talent for impersonations. Then there was Walter Gunning with his bigger than life personality imitating "The Three Stooges" perfectly.

Sophomore Year

In the Fall of her sophomore year, Virginia would lose another of her classmates - Judy Osier. She was a pleasnat, upbeat gal who corresponded with Virginia regularly when she was in the hospital. Her coloring was jaundiced. Virginia got out of school to go to her funeral. God rest Judy.

Annie was always coming home from school with stories. Seems they were studying about different cultures in other countries where worms were eaten as part of the diet. One girl piped up, "That ain't nothing, my Uncle eats raw hamburg!"

Virginia was fond of Mr. Royce, her history teacher. He taught American History. Only Virginia did something on a dare that she is ashamed of to this day. When she was a candystriper, the orderly at the hospital told her that she should write "WWII Charlie" on the chalkboard. He told her that the teacher would like that. Being immature, she thoughtlessly did. This must have hurt him. She has regretted it ever since. Kids do things for attention or Lord knows what. She would go on to make baked goods for Mr. Royce and visit him and correspond with him when as she continued to grow and afterward when she finished school.

Mr. Cembalski

Mr. Cembalski taught Virginia Geometry. Annie always liked him as a teacher. She would come home and tell stories. He had a quiet, gentle way about him. He would make one think of Clarence on "It's a Wonderful Life". Although he failed Virginia because she did not grasp the concepts, she took it again the following year. One day her nose would not stop running, Mr. Cembalski thoughtfully gave her some tissues. On another occasion he questioned what happened to her as he noticed a large pimple on her face. He was trying to give her some fatherly advice but it left Virginia mortified. Nonetheless, she had tremendous respect for this teacher. She would see him at church with his family. She had heard that he was thinking of the priesthood. Sometimes Virginia would ask her Uncle H.G. to help her with the Math. Well, it was very satisfying when one day, it all started to click. When the student began to focus and set aside her lofty dreams, it all came together. Later, she would share with this teacher how she would like to write a book. He used to ask her how it was coming; only, it was not coming. She told him when it does, she would dedicate it to him.

Virginia did spread herself kind of thin with all the activities in which she was involved. Evidently, she missed a prom decorating meeting. Virginia was class secretary. The class president called her on this. Virginia was taken aback as she did not realize there was a meeting that she was supposed to attend. When Lynn caught wind of this, she came to Virginia's defense. Lynn was good like that.

On the way back from candystriping , Virginia would make the rounds and visit different folks around town. She would stop at Lord Howe Street, not far from the monument, and visit Maud Leach and Eva Carter. Maud is the one who worked for Virginia's father's family for years. They had the homiest of homes though these ladies did not have much in the material sense. Great Aunt Mary used to say that if something happened to Uncle Donald that she would like to go and live with them. Whatever these ladies did have, they would share with their young visitor. Maud was practically blind then. Grampa used to get Bing cherries for Maud when they were in season as she loved them. These Christian women gave young Virginia a mustard seed pendant which has remained a treasure for her.

Virginia used to visit Great Aunt Mary and Uncle Donald regularly. She would often join them for dinner. There would be Harvard beets, macaroni and cheese and filets of fish. Great -Aunt Mary was a good cook same as her sister, Grandmother Audette. They gave little Virginia an engraved sterling silver candlestick for Christmas one year.

Virginia made lots of friends with folks recuperating at the hospital. One was an elderly blind man - Mr. Breed. She continued to visit him at his house when he returned home. She also cut his grass. She felt bad because later she came to realize that a neighborhood boy used to cut it. She feared she had taken his job without intending to.

Save Me a Seat

The teenager cherished her rest. She would stay up very late doing homework. Consequently, it was difficult to get up in the morning. Though, once up, she could get going in record time. She would walk through the back lot, and up Amherst Avenue to the school. One winter morning, Lizzy decided to play a trick on her. She told her that it was a "snow day" when in fact it was not. Virginia rolled over and went back to sleep. Later, she did get to school - marked tardy.

One tradition that Lizzy started was when all the children went to bed at night, they would say to each other, "Save me a seat on the bus to dreamland" followed by, "next to the window."

Sometimes Virginia would help the school nurse in the morning in the nurse's office. This meant she had to get to school ealrier. She was accustomed to getting there just before the bell would ring at 8:44 a.m.

She enjoyed the lunches in high school too. They were forty cents then. The lunch ladies were very good to Virginia. She made a point to be the last one in line as that would ensure an extra helping of mashed potato or something. Mrs. Letson always gave her an extra large piece of the lemon cake.

Jim Curio would ask the spirited teen to go out to Stewart's for an ice cream or maybe go swimming at his house. Sometimes she would stay for dinner. Jim's father was real jovial. His mother thought the teenager was using him. This never occurred to her. She was happy-go-lucky and liked everybody. Grampa said that she was hopelessly naive. "Everyone is not a nice guy." He would say to her.

She went to three of the proms in high school. John Oakes took her in the tenth grade. It rained very heavily - flooding nearby Amherst Avenue. Norman Blaise, also known as "Sunshine" took her the junior year. He was a likeable fellow who loved motorcycles and the band called "The Eagles". Henry and Thomas were good friends with Norman. Norman took Virginia out to Thatchers Olde School House Restaurant on Street Road before the prom. Chuck Kelly took Virginia in her senior year. That was the year that she wore the mink stole that Mrs. Jane King, the pharmacist's wife, had given her.

Speaking of Jane King, one time Virginia met her second oldest son Billy at the parade. He was either in Karl or Georgie's class - at least four years Virginia's senior. He must have thought the girl to be older than what she was. He called her up one time. For privacy, she took the call at the big house. Of course Uncle H.G. knew everything because he used to work for the CIA. Then when Billy met her, he seemed embarrassed when he learned that she was only sixteen. He did not want to be seen with her. They were both hiding out on Uncle Charlie's porch. It was kind of funny. His mother worked for Uncle Charlie - Dr. Walsh. She also helped out in the office for Doctor Tom. Billy was very witty and he resembled John Lennon. His older brother Joe used to work at the Fort for Grampa. Joe really admired him. He often reminisces aobut those Fort Days with the Audette men. Joe wrote for a column for an Albany newspaper.

There was a parish "Dime a dip" Supper one time and Mrs. King made some goulash in her mother's favorite pot. One of the parish ladies took the leftovers home. Billy was charged with the task of retrieving the pot from Mrs. Murphy. He went to her house and Mrs. Murphy said, "I will get it. Just let me remove my underwear that I have been boiling in the pot." "That's okay, you can keep it." Billy replied.

Ice Cream on the Fly

One story Virginia remembers her father telling was when this Japanese tourist came in to the log house where the soda fountain was right before closing. It had been a long day. He wanted a chocolate ice cream cone. My father scooped up some Hood's chocolate ice cram from teh big cylinder cardboard container. The scoop of ice cream slid off the cone, onto the counter, making its way to the floor. Daddy plucked that ball of ice cream up off the floor and plopped it back onto the cone and presented it to the baffled customer. Then, he and his Uncle Cyrus retreated to the kitchen in hysterics. Henry always got a kick out of the way father told this story.

Virginia could and would tell her mother anything and everything. She had a wonderful open dialogue with her. Even when her friend Lynn wanted to sneak out, she consulted with her mother. Then she thought better of it and needless to say, she did not go out.

The Dutch Touch

The Van Dirks and the teRieles were a large Dutch family coming over from Holland. Ted teRiele would bring liver from his cows for Mrs. Audette. The Van Dirks were a big farming family. They were hard working people with a strong Faith. Mrs. Van Dirk would make you think of Queen Elizabeth. Gramma Farleigh did too for that matter. They both bore that regal countenance. They loaned their daughters' long dresses to the Audette girls for different functions. One of the boys had stepped on a rusty nail. He got lockjaw. The prognosis was not good. The family prayed the Rosary. Young Jim rallied. It is said that he had a supernatural experience. One can conclude this by the manner that Jim lives as he is a very Godly man.

Aunt Betty

Gramma Farleigh was born in October so she could justifiably wear opal. She was way ahead of her times. Doctor J P Cummins wanted to sponsor her for Medical School. She would have made a great doctor. She raised her family of nine. Her second youngest, was, Betty. She was special. The doctors did not think that she would live to ten years of age. The family did not think that they would have her for long. Hence she was spoiled. Betty was predictable in that she was unpredictable. She made it to Seventy-Five! She was savant. She could put together 5,000 piece puzzles like no one's business. She could put things together literally and figuratively. She knew things before they happened. If you did not finish a sentence, then, Aunt Betty would finish it for you. She knew what you were thinking. She knew when people died before anyone else did. Father O'Reilly used to say that Aunt Betty was like a barometer for how people felt at large. She would go into deep mourning on the death of an acquaintance or that of a celebrity. The "Beatles" musical group affected her most deeply as Betty was a Beatles aficionado from the get-go. She had every paraphernalia that was ever made associated with the Beatles. So it was a given that Betty would have her "funeral face" on when John Lennon died. Don't say Paul McCartney without according hism his knighted title of "Sir"! She could be very exacting. One time, as Gramma Farleigh was pulling out onto the road, she asked her daughter if any cars were coming. "No Mother," Betty replied, "just a truck." Gramma hits the breaks!

Gramma was dedicated to the "March of Dimes" knowing firsthand the travails of raising one with special needs. Betty sure made life colorful. It was marvelous how Gramma raised her. She refused to have her daughter institutionalized. Gramma helped found the ARC where Betty would go to learn skills. Indeed, the local ARC is named for her. Betty had a large vocabulary. Gramma saw to it that Betty got her hair done every Friday at the hairdressers. Gramma ordered her the best clothes from the catalogues. Betty did not have any gray hairs. Aunt Jane suggested that she gave them to everyone.

In many ways, Aunt Betty was like an older sister to the Audette children. When the Audette girls would break out in nervous laughter or at an inopportune time, Betty would chime in laughing hysterically.

Betty did not like pennies. She really had an aversion to them. She was very generous by nature though she had little concept of money. She might give you a twenty dollar bill and ask you to pick her up a bottle of Pepsi telling you to keep the change. At the same time, she might give you a couple of quarters for the same bottle and it might not cover it but you would still be told to keep the change. One thing that sticks out in Little Virginia's mind is that when she was a little girl, Aunt Betty took her down to Newberry's and bought her a little see-through plastic purse with novelties in it for her birthday.

Besides the Beatles, Betty's favorite things begin with the letter "P". There was Pepsi, Pizza and Pasta. Her mother was very good about teaching her moderation in all things. One time, Ringo Starr was playing in Albany. Gramma saw to it that Betty got to go. In fact, Little Virginia took her.

Aunt Sue

Betty liked ot be called "Aunt Sue". One day she was talking on the phone with her niece Jane. Jane was talking to Sue Huestis on another line. Then she said, "Bah Sue" - only she said it to Aunt Betty's line. Aunt Betty thought that was hysterical. From then on, she insisted that everyone call her "Aunt Sue".

Betty adored her mother. She looked up to her like a puppy. When they were eating, a particle of food might fall on Grandmother's blouse. Aunt

Betty would point this out to her, "Mother, you have something right there." If Virginia and her sisters were there, there would be stifled laughter. This would bring on a huge smile from Betty bursting into laughter. Annie always said that Gramma and Uncle H.G. took their laughter in stride. They knew there was no malicious intent.

Aunt Betty had a lifelike doll. She named him "Thomas". Whenever anyone entered the big house, they were hushed to be quiet because Thomas was sleeping in the nearby basinette. Aunt Betty had the strongest maternal instinct. She lived for babies. If she were to trip and fall holding a baby, that baby would still be cradled and clutched in her arms. She was fiercely protective. Although, she will remind everyone of the time that she dropped her baby brother Sherrie from the couch.

Uncle H.G.

Gramma lost her husband to a heart attack when he was only 59 years old. A year later, she lost her second youngest son to an automobile accident. Johnny was only 20 years old - a fine-looking fellow. All the aunts and uncles were smart. They all went to college and earned teaching degrees. Uncle H.G. was in the CIA when he was in the Army. He was a quiet, thoughtful man - the oldest of Gramma and Gransier Farleigh's chidlren. He was the mainstay for Gramma after Gransieur died. uncle H.G. was incredible. He did so much for so many that no one ever knew about. He was like his uncle who was a school teacher. Great Uncle John Cunningham was a school teacher too. He would look out for his students who might come from a family who did not have much in the material sense. H.G. was like this and he particularly looked out for those who might not have a father or kids from a single parent home.

H.G. knew Lake George like the back of the palm of his hand. He was a pilot on the Mohigan. He also was a referee for different high school sports. He was a daily communicant at church. One time, little Virginia mentioned that her paternal grandfather was looking for a grey zip up sweater to keep him warm in the winter. Not a week went by and Grampa Audette received one in the mail from L.L. Bean.

One of the greatest moments Virginia shared with her uncle was when Gramma asked her how this one elderly lady who she took care of was doing. This lady who went to school with H.G. was assisting her too. It seems she fell asleep while the poor elderly woman was lying on the floor calling for help. The more Virginia elaborated, the funnier it got. Uncle H.G. looked at his mother, and he just convulsed with laughter. Gramma Farleigh shared a hearty laugh too. When folks share a good belly laugh together, it is bonding.

Cousins

Aunt Mary and Uncle Mike lived in a college town in the Mohawk Valley. They would come to Ticonderoga on holidays and many weekends throughout the year. During the summer, they would take some of the Audette children back with them to visit. They had three sons who were really more like brothers to the Audette children. There was Thomas, Michael and Stephen. Virginia named one of the Pagan Babies after Stephen when whe was in the 7th grade. She received five dollars for her Confirmation which she could not wait to give to the Pagan Baby Association. She was rewarded with naming the baby. Somewhere in Africa there is a Stephen Andrew running around.

Aunt Mary's kids had nicknames too. Michael was called "Mootsie". He spells it "Mootse". Stephen was called "Scrubs". Not sure about Tom. They had a great dog - a beagle mix the boys name "Grover" - she was a girl so it was 'G' plus 'Rover'. A lot of fun was had with the McDonalds. Aunt Mary and Uncle Mike were very generous to the Audette family. They would order pizza and treat the kids to a movie or take them to Hot Gene's in Port Henry for a Michigan hot dog. One time on little Virginia' birthday, they asked her what her favorite meal would be and what kind of cake. She was turning fourteen. She chose stew and spice cake. Uncle Mike was a great cook. It turned out delicious. They helped Mrs. Audette out at Christmas with gifts for all the children. Uncle Mike was a lawyer. he was also a man of principle and integrity. Unfortunately, where politics are involved, that is not popular. Hard times befell him. He served his country in the Army. That is probably where he was given cigarettes. He later got Cancer. God rest Uncle Mike.

Aunt Mary

Doesn't everyone have an "Aunt Mary"? If they don't, they should have. Aunt Mary was a lot of fun growing up. She used to give the kids "airplane rides" same as her little brother Sherrie did. She would drive barefoot in the summer and swing her hands as the radio blared "Ain't Got No Cigarettes". She was a cute blonde cheer leader. She has these blue eyes which some family members likened to "Betty Davis eyes". Daddy got a kick out of that song which amused cousin Michael. Aunt Mary is devout in her prayers. She is a daily communicant at Mass. She does the tithe in reverse. She probably gives 90 per cent of what she has to the missions and to others.   Aunt Mary is the most generous person in the world. She enjoys going out to eat and she likes gourmet food. She is very family-oriented. At 85 years of age, she like her younger sister Betty, does not have a gray hair on her head. Then Gramma Farleigh's hair was brown up into her 90's. Gramma Farleigh should have been the spokesperson for Pond's cold cream. She used it every day. She had the most beautiful skin. She looked fabulous at 100 when Our Good Lord called her home.

Of Pecuniary Ways

The worse thing in life is to be pecuniary. One thing is to be frugal and not live beyond one's means, but another is to be downrigh cheap. Not all people are going to be equally as giving. It depends on how secure one feels. There was this one woman who used to book Virginia six months in advance to babysit on New Year's Eve. It was hard to get out of it and if was difficult for the youngster to say no to people. This woman only paid her fifty cents an hour. On top of that, the girl was uncomfortable in the house because there was this big Siberian Husky who use to stare at Virginia. He would not take his eyes off her. Granted he had the most beautiful blue eyes. She dared not take a piece of fudge out of the candy dish. There would be no enjoying it. Then, Virginia was warned that she better not fall asleep. The woman and her husband did not get home until after 2 a.m.! People should treat people the way they themselves would like to be treated.

Where Clutter Abounds

Unless you were Aunt Jane who was in the convent and lived the vow of poverty, clutter seems to an affiction that assails the Farleigh family. It comes with being hopelessly sentimental. Grampa Audette would accuse little Virginia of saving a toothpick from a restaurant. This is an exaggeration though his granddaughter did save paper clippings and mementos from wherever she went. She would make scrap books. Then newspapers pile up before they get a chance to be clipped. Oh, and do you remember that magazine article?! This is long before storing files on a chip came to be. Hence growing up in the Audette household was a bit cluttered if embarrassing. Perhaps it was the litmus test because one really did not feel comfortable to have anyone in the house. If someone entered, that someone was in a rare comfort zone of trust. There would be no blurting out how "accumulated" the Audettes were! Grampa Audette used to say that old Sheridan Farleigh was probably buried under a stack of mother's New York Times in her sitting room.

The family grew up on hand-me-downs. It is nearly impossible for any of the siblings to pass a thrift store without going in. Sure they might be dropping a bag off, but they are more likely to leave with twice what they brought in. The interesting thing is, on any given Saturday morning, one can find two ro more of the Audette girls at the Methodist Thrift store. They all gravitate towards the same items. Generally it is blue and white dishes. The Blue Willow evokes a lot of memories. They like a nice percolator, or a tea cup or an old souvenir plate from "Story Town". Life is short. They have good taste.   Might just as well enjoy these ditties.

Loyalty

They all stick together and they all understand each other. Aunt Betty taught them about loyalty early on. She was loyal to the core -

instinctively. Her biggest fear was letting her mother down. She adored her mother. One time, on her birthday, she woke up, came downstairs in her bathrobe, and announced, "Today is my birthday and I am wearing my birthday suit!" Then she proceded to open her robe. Gramma got such a kick out of this.

It is no wonder that mother's siblings were generous. They had only to take a cue from their mother. When Gramma was widowed, she continued to work hard in the Paper Mill Office downtown. She was good with figures. She also worked as a docent at Fort Ticonderoga when she was well in her eighties. She would wear the long Colonial dress and stand for over eight hours a day in the museum. Gramma was always writing out cards and putting checks in them. One man was in a burn accident. Gramma sent him a card to lift his spirits and she enclosed a generous check. She was giving away her hard earned money just as quickly as it came in. She had thousands of Masses offered up for her brethren. She kept going. She had a routine and yet, ahead of her time, she managed to travel the world. She visited Aunt Jane in the Solomon Islands when Aunt Jane was doing missionary work there. She visited The Holy Land. She toured Europe. She kissed the Blarney Stone in Cork, Ireland. She went to Hawaii. She made spiritual retreats every year. She loved to travel. Moreover, Gramma was not afraid of anyone or anything. She prayed a lot and she went to Mass daily.

At times, perhaps, the Audettes may hae felt a little taken for granted. There was so many of them and they happened to live next door. They were expected to clean and move things or do heavy lifting that they would never dare ask any of the other relatives. It was a good feeling to be comfortable but a left-handed compliment when asked to clean up after the visiting relatives' dog messed on the Oriental rug! It made them who they were and hopefully for the better as a result.

Getting the house ready for those annual book club meetings was something else. This is where the lace curtain Irish came through. There was silver to be polished. There was an air of tension as prepartions were under way. Mrs. Yeanney's daffodil cake with lemon sauce had to be picked up. The cucumber and potted ham tea sandwiches had to be made.　　　　　　Pepperidge Farm cookies were put on a silver tray. Linens were used. Greet the ladies at the door, take their coats and replenish the tea. Oh yes, and when Mrs. MacMilan from Hague inadvertently locks herself in the bathroom, summon help!

The "Killer Aunts"

Aunt Anne was another one of mother's siblings. She came after Aunt Mary. She married Uncle Mike's brothers. His name was John. He was very big. He was "Big John". When the Audette children were little, if they were offered something to eat or drink, they used to reply, "I don't care." This really meant yes, but just in case there was not enough and to protect from rejection, this was the standard and safe reply. This used to annoy Aunt Anne. "Why can't they just say yes, or no." She would exclaim. She was right. There is something in the Good Book about this. The children have since learned to be less tentative. Virginia used to accompany Lizzy when she used to babysit for the cousins. She was wearing one blue sock and one black sock. Uncle John said, "Little Virginia, I bet you have another pair just like them at home." Virginia blushed. Lizzy used to call Uncle John "Pinhead". He had a crewcut and he was a big man. He was big in more ways than one. He was the district attorney. He has a big heart; and, he knew what his nieces and nephews called him. He took it all in stride. He was always helping the family get out of scrapes. Aunt Anne is very active in politics. She belongs to various elite clubs. She earned the moniker "Queen Anne". She is very well-read. No one takes advantage of her. She sort of puts up a barrier, but underneath, she is very sensitive and good. She has a special bond with Virginia's sister Jane. Jane does a lot for her. She cleans her house and gets her camp ready in the Spring. Aunt Anne and Uncle John have three children who are double cousins to Aunt Mary and Uncle Mike's children. They have all done very well for themselves. One of them, was affectionately called "Cousin It" - this only because her beautiful, long blonde hair nearly went 360 degrees around her head. Cousin It was the character in the tv sitcom 'The Adams Family' and "It" had a lot of hair.

Another cousin is Joseph. He is Aunt Jane's son. He was the most beautiful baby. His father was from the Solomon Islands. He was an important head of state there. Joseph has the sweetest voice. He sings at church at all the weddings and funerals. He is closest in age to the baby of the Audette family - Sarah. However, he and Virginia did a lot of fun things together.

Paternal Family

There is another set of double cousins on Virginia's father's side of the family. That is, grandfather Audette married grandmother Ferris. Her sister, great-Aunt Mary, married great Uncle Donald Audette. Hence father, his sister Karlene and Uncle Cyrus are first double cousins to the children of Great Aunt Mary and great Uncle Donald.

Uncle Donald had beagles. He would take them for runs up on Warner Hill. They would find rabbits.

Grandfather Audette had another brother named Desmond. He was sharp with a keen mathematical mind. He was married to a very attractive lady. They had five children and they ran a hotel downtown across from where the bank is. In 1959, there was a tragic fire that broke out in the hotel. Great Uncle Desmond went in to get his sixteen year-old daughter Michelle. It was too late for both of them. There was a third victim too. It was Ticonderoga's darkest hour. One of the tenants had fallen asleep in a chair with a cigarette.

Grampa had a sister Dorcas too. She lived next door to the Audettes on Champlain Avenue. Aunt Dorcas crocheted the Audette girls cloche hats for Christmas one year. Aunt Dorcas had these bright brown eyes like Grampa's. She was very stylish. Her husband was a doctor. He made house calls same as did Doctor Tom and all the local doctors. Her daughter, Cousin Ann, would cut the girls hair. Ann is Virginia's Godmother. Grampa nicknamed Ann "Root Beer". Her brother Jimmy was Virginia's Godfather. Ann worked with her Uncle Karl at the Fort in the summer. She was cute and full of life. Grampa got a kick out of her.

These cousins were very loyal to Grampa - their Uncle Karl. Dr. Walsh was called "Uncle Charlie" by the Audette children. Not sure why because his name was "James". Uncle Charlie was stricken with Diabetes later on. He lost a leg. Virginia used to visit him in the nursing home before he was transferred to a facility in Brattleboro, Vermont. When Aunt Dorcas died, the Audette boys were pallbearers. Cousin John Audette was also a pallbearer. He seemed to be a professional pallbearer. One of the nuns was doing a reading. It seems one of her legs was shorter than the other. Cousin John asked brother Karl what her name was. Karl replied, "Sister Eileen". Uncontrollable laughter ensued in the first two pews on the left side in Saint Mary's that day.

Uncle Cyrus

Uncle Cyrus was the most fun loving and generous person. Virginia adored him. He was an excellent mimic. He had a great sense of humor to match. When he was a little boy, he went to the school on the other side of Carillon Road. It was Alexandria School. He would come home for lunch and more often than not, he would spend the rest of the day home with his mother. Gramma seemed to like this as she never encouraged him to go back. He served in the Air Force during the Viet Nam War. He was stationed in Thailand. He was very devoted to his parents. He wrote regularly sending home souvenirs. He had to take off some weight before joining the Service. He took off a vast amount of weight in a short time. He went on some sort of grapefruit diet. Gramma Audette was an excellent cook. She spared no ingredients when she cooked. She cooked in the style of those two English ladies known as "The Two Fat Ladies". Cyrus would take Virginia out and teach her how to drive. He loved taking his family out to dinner. He was so bighearted. He would check on his parents every day. He was very sentimental. He would come to the Audette house when the kids were little. He and Daddy would be in the cellar imitating John Wayne. They recorded their antics on a tape recorder. He gave Virginia her first tape recorder. Grampa gave Virginia her first cassette - Loretta Lynn - Harper Valley PTA. Grampa loved that.

Daddy's sister lived up North so the Audettes did not see her often. She only got home a couple of times a year. She went to the same school in Troy as her mother did. There is a newspaper clipping of Gramma Audette wearing a racoon coat going for a sled ride down on the hill on the grounds of Emma Willard. Aunt Karlene was very sharp. She did two years of business school at Mildred Elly in one. She was a real beauty too though she nearly died young. Dr. Walsh helped save her.

It is painful to think what Gramma and Grampa Audette went through when their son, Virginia's father, was shot in the eye with a B B gun. He was driven to specialists in Boston. He endured painful injections. He had Glaucoma and he nearly lost his eyesight completely. He did lose eyesight in his right eye. What a heartbreak for his parents.

One thing that sticks out in Virginia's mind is how her father told of two of his comrades in the Service (Air Force) were agreed to meet ten years later in Times Square. Virginia would have gladly gone as his emissary as she is a romantic. Even if no one was there, she would have like to have attempted it. Life happens when plans are made.

Junior Year

One crisp Autumn day, Virginia and Lynn made plans to ride their bikes to Shoreham, Vermont. They would pick apples. They would take the Ferry over. They made bologna sandwiches, packed them in "Tuperware" and got their backpacks and headed down the Fort Road. They got on the Ferry going over Lake Champlain into Vermont. It was a Sunday,a school night, and it was taking a lot longer to get to the orchard than they figured. Before they knew it, it was dark. "What are we going to do Lynn?" Virginia asked her friend. So they knocked at a house close to the ferry landing. It was the operator of the ferry. He had been keeping an eye out for the vagabonds. He very kindly took over on the ferry. It was around 9 p.m. He was duly compensated in apples.

Another time, the two Juniors had heard about "Senior Skip Day". They thought it would be fun to take the day off too. They got the

"Tupperware" out and packed a lunch and headed for the beach. Later, they did a little sun tanning on the upper deck of Lynn's family home. No one was home that day. They almost got away with it. They were casually walking down Black Point Road, when all of a sudden, the distinctive sound of that Black Beard's muffler on that Volkswagon truck could be heard. The girls were near the Van Zuphten's house. There was a steep embankment on the left side of the road. What to do! Before they could cross over and hide, a deep voice was heard, "Get in." Lynn and Virginia got in and were talking silly gibberish. In retrospect, father must have seen himself in such an escapade. He must have gotten a kick out of it. Anyway, Virginia was grounded.

That did not stop Virginia from making a coffee table for her father for Christmas. She was taking a wood working class. She saved up to buy the lumber. She could not have been prouder. She put a big red bow on it. Her brothers helped her hide it in the dining room on Christmas Eve. Father was very pleased. He was very sentimental too.

Vacuum Cleaners

Virginia has a fondness for vacuum cleaners. She picked up a 1932 Hoover at the Church of The Cross Bazaar for four dollars. It had a great heavy motor and a thick cloth bag. It was an upright vacuum. In an effort to de-clutter, she got rid of it (that which she regrets). Funny enough,, when her father was little, he would not go to the store with his mother unless he could take the vacuum cleaner with him. Karl saw this handy little car vacuum. He wanted to give it to mother and father for their fifteenth wedding anniversary. It was a red plastic device that ran on batteries. The kids pitched in. This would clean up the wood paneled Ford station wagon.

Then there was the "Dirt Devil". Grampa liked throwing that name around. Annie and Virginia were visiting Grampa when he was expounding how it worked. The two sisters just looked at each other and they could not stop laughing. Grampa ran with it and further embellished his story. He always enjoyed a good audience.

Breaker, Breaker

Daddy was funny if not eccentric. He enjoyed Jonathan Winters. They were remarkably similar. When CB Radio first came out, he jumped on the "band" wagon so to speak. His handle was "Black Beard" of course. He got right into the jargon. "Breaker, Breaker, Black Beard here....." "Well, that's a big negatory", "Roger that," "That's a big ten four". He would take drives mostly just to go out and converse on the CB radio. He enjoyed going to the Ferry Landing or boat launch. The Audette men could wear beards as four generations have attested.

Thomas was the real "Ten Four". That was his weight at birth. Mary was a good-sized baby too weighing in at nine pounds, four ounces.

Daddy had a nice bar in the cellar. All the kids' school pictures were hung up behind it. His father also had a bar in his cellar so it was only natural. Karl would follow suit. This one man who lived on Amherst Avenue used to come over a lot. His name was George Clemons. He had a daughter Annie's age. Karl made homemade root beer in the cellar. Then he moved on and brewed beer. He really has an entrepeneruical mind.

In addition the father's mancave, Daddy had a "Field Office". This was an old school bus that he bought somewhere. He had this situated on the lake lot tht Nana Farleigh had given to Mother. It was comical if a bit of an eyesore. But inside, was a thermos of coffee and a view of Roger's Slide to be had. Life was good for Black Beard on Black Point Road.

Father was not the only eccentricity on Black Point Road. Long time ago, lived old Mrs. Newell. She had a white house where Uncle Tommy's log camp is now. She drove an old black Model T Ford. She would remind one of "Granny on the Hillbillies".

Then there was the summer resident who came from the city. He was a coach who ran a boys camp. He used to be in the Marines. His name was

Baker. One day, Mr. Baker drove off the seawall in Burleigh Bay. Thank God he was okay - minor injuries.

Go parrallel two roads over on the Hague Road, and there was Clyde Bligh. This local legend built his own car out of wood and whatever he came up with. When the Audette children were little, they would sit with the neighbors on the black bar in front of Walshs. They would watch traffic go by. Then, there it was - Clyde Bligh's contraption in all its glory. It never disappoints. What he lacked in the material sense, he made up for with ingenuity.

Senior Year

Virginia and Lynn were in the Junior Miss Program their senior year. Lynn loved ballet. She dance to Swan Lake. Virginia did a take-off from "Funny Girl". She sang, or tried to, "I'm The Greatest Star". She even had a sweatshirt made with that on it for the logo. She did receive an award for talent. Sloan Wilson said she was the best one.

One of her most memorable moments on stage in high school was when the Stony Brook Jazz Ensemble came to town. They were going to do an Assembly at school when they met Virginia. She was practicing her dancing at Betty Wilson's studio. They were staying in the loft that Betty's father had built. The manager was called 'Dragon Lady'. She was from the Orient. There were some Black musicians. They all made Virginia feel like she was a movie star already. Then, Dragon Lady made a proposition. "How would you like to dance in one of the numbers tomorrow?" 'Lo and behold, when the Charleston came on, Virginia fluttered on stage with Mrs. Malaney's black satin fringed flapper dress. The classmates were all cheering in disbelief. The timing was on point. She would repeat this that evening. However, her timing was off.

Shortly after the Assembly, Virginia was humming in art class. The teacher was annoyed with her. "Shut up!" He hollared at her. "Just because you did some ditty on stage, you think you are pretty special." The girl was stunned. No one had ever bursted her bubble like that.

Meekly, she kept still. Marge Murphy went out of her way to say that her act was not good. Virginia expected that, just not from a teacher. Perhaps life was difficult for him on the homefront. God Bless him.

Tupperware

Lynn's mother boasted that "Tupperware" is the Cadillac fo plastics. She herself was the queen of Tupperware. She would attend these conventions in Albany regularly. All her tasty baked goodies were stored in these containers. One time Virginia had a tupperware party for Mrs. Clarke. Mrs. Clarke let her hold it at her house. Mrs. Clarke was a beautiful woman and she was very maternal. She was also a great seamstress. She sewed a swimsuit for Lynn and she also made one for her friend. She knitted mittens for Lynn and again, she knitted a pair for Virginia. She knitted Virginia's nickname on them: "The Virg". It was a take off from that show called 'The Happy Days' - it had that character "The Fonz".

Lynn's Dad would collect the sap from the maple trees and boil it down to make maples syrup. Mrs. Clarke used this when she made Lynn her birthday cakes. He was a Colonel in the Army. He helped deliver babies in Germany during the second World War. He regaled in telling war stories. He was a real character. He had a great sense of humor. Virginia loved Lynn's father. He was very kind to her. All Lynn's family were very smart and they did well. Most of them went to Cornell University. Becky went to Dartmouth though. Debbie was very cool and clever. Lynn's family took Virginia with them when they went to New York to visit Debbie. Virginia was in awe of her apartment. There was a huge black and white print of an old car on the wall.

Alice the Cat

Besides their beagle Wilbur, the Audettes had a black Angorra cat they named Alice. She had a lovely temperament. The children used to tell their mother that she reminded them of Alice. It was meant as a compliment because Mother was calm and easy-going. The janitor from the high school, Joe Izzo, visited Mother at the hospital after she had a surgery. He told her that she might put on some weight because his cat put on weight after a similar surgery.

Swimming on The Point

Great Aunt Mary and Uncle Donald summered at their camp on the Point. It was like a peninsula. It was a beautiful, private spot. They lost a daughter in a drowning accident. It happened in Lake Luzerne. Father had to go to identify his first double cousin. Cousin John went too. Two daughters were left without a mother. They had the same names as Virginia's older sisters: Annie and Lizzy. Gramma Audette always had a soft spot for her niece, the girls' mother. The girls would spend a lot of time with their grandparents. Virginia got to know them. They would have fun together, visiting and sharing their dreams. One day Cousin Annie and Virginia arranged to take their respective grandmothers to lunch at Stewarts. The girls were going to treat their grandmothers. Gramma Audette discreetly took the bill. Little Virginia did not realize that Gramma Audette was not well at the time. Grampa and Daddy did not feel that she was up to going out. Later Grampa told his granddaughter how much she enjoyed that. She loved to get out and go for rides which she often did with her sons.

Gramma and Grampa Audette also had a camp near the Point. However, Grampa suffered an excruciating ear infection one summer. It put him right off of even wanting to stay near the lake.

Pondering

It is disappointing in life when one party is loyal and steadfast in friendship while the other becomes fairweathered. One has reached out, sending gifts without them being acknowledged. People go through things in life. Generally, when people go through a crisis, they are receptive when one reaches out to them. Others are uncomfortable for whatever reason. They prefer their safe, secure spot and the door is closed save for a crack.

Caveat: Did you know that the green-eyed monster lurks?

Run, Virginia, Run

Virginia began running when she was fourteen years old. Of course she was always running to and from the big house when she was little. She would run over six miles a day - up to the beach and back on Black Point Road. She was the first female to take up running in Ticonderoga. She was the only female to run in the ten mile club that Spring. Coach Stevenson followed her with a car suggesting that it was okay to get in and ride the rest of the way back to the school. Nothin' doin'! This must be the strong will that Father Halligan was referring to. Grampa's neighbor was the boys track coach. He would run in the Boston Marathon. One neighborhood girl named Leslie used admire the muscles that developed in Virginia's legs. Gramma Audette did not know what to make of this running business.

Bicentennial Year

It was the Summer of 1976. Virginia had not quite turned sixteen. She was laying on her cot. She could not stop crying. She had just learned that her Grandmother Audette died. She had just had a Schweppes gingerale with her the previous day after her jog. She noticed that her grandmother was raising her left arm up. She had no idea what she was going through. Gramma had Congestive Heart Failure. Grampa knew if the shade was up, it would be alright. This morning, the shade had not been drawn. Grampa had just finished working his night shift at the hospital as a security guard. He dreaded going in the house. He knew what it meant. He called Doctor Tom. Gramma would sleep in her chair as it made breathing easier. Little Virginia used to hover behind her when she visited. So much was felt, but unspoken. Grampa would not go to the funeral home. He did go to the Church of The Cross. Gramma's family donated the large Crucifix behind the Altar. Gramma was fond of Reverend Kermit Castellanos. He did the funeral. Virginia was sitting in the pew behind Grampa. He turned around and cupped her hands. The last time Virginia saw Gramma and Grampa together in church was at Ann

Walsh's wedding. Virginia thought she should go since she is Ann's Goddaughter. Virginia was wearing that Best & Company dress that her mother had gotten for eachof the seven girls for Christmas. It had a red, white and blue grosgrain ribbon down the center and a small, neat bow on top in the middle of the neckline. Grampa was making those same sounds that he made when he was getting the squirrels to come and eat from his hands. He was moitioning for the child to come and sit with them. Little Virginia turned and smiled shyly at them.

Virginia did go to work that day. She was selling ice cream at the Fort. Madge, her boss, said, "Virgey (as she only called her), why did you come into work today? You didn't have to." But Virginia did not know what to do. She was too scared to call in and then she would not have made it through the phone call. She went in the next day too. She held in all the pain and smiled. Customers even remarked on her cheerful disposition. Of course Madge said that 'Virgey' could sell ice cream to the Eskimos. Virginia did not go in to work on the day of the funeral. She rode her bike up to the lake later that day. She went swimming at Aunt Mary and Uncle Donald's. Aunt Mary looked at her, "I love you Deary."

On the Audette childrens' birthda;ys, Grandmother would take each and everyone down to Cooke & Sacco's to get a new birthday outfit and a new pair of PF Flyer sneakers. In the latter years she gave cards with money. Often the kids would show up on their birthdays not realizing that Gramma knew why they were there. They were looking for their birthday card. Virginia treasures a birthday card that that Gramma Audette gave her when she turned 12. It came from Bunny's corner drugstore. It said, "Sugar and Spice, and everything nice, That's You Honey....."

When Virginia was in the fifth grade, she made Gramma a present.. She took a yellow empty Joy dish detergent bottle. She cut a piece of red gingham fabric and put a shawl around it. She glued an apron on it and made earrings out of pipe cleaners. She put a kerchief on the round black glass head which she affixed. Grampa told Virginia how much Gramma loved that. She had treasures from the Orient: Persian carpets, bronze sculptures, oil paintings and priceless candlebra. Yet this very humble gift received a place of honor in her home. Virginia also use to give Gramma gifts that she won from her Christmas seals that she sold from school. A plastic Nativity or a statue of Our Blessed Mother. These took precedence over her Hummels.

The Good Reverend

"Kermit" as he was universally called, could be likened to Saint Nicholas. He would make these little gifts out of wood from his carpenter's shop: Oranments, Nativities, toaster tongs little plaques with verses and so on. Then, he would have parties in teh summer. he would invite all the children who lived around the lake near where he lived. He was well loved. Gramma Audette was very fond of him. Going to Saint Mary's, Virginia did not meet him until she was in high school. She sometimes rode her bike up the Baldwin Road. That is when she met him. He learned of her desire for the stage. He had a church in California where many actors and actresses went. His good friend, Mary Wickes, the character actress was coming for a visit. He invited Virginia for dinner so that she could meet her. Kermit grilled some steak and made cole slaw. Virginia brought cheesecake. It was from a box mix. Her cousin Nancy Kingsley taught her how to make it. She also brought her autograph book which Mary Wickes graciously signed.

Kermit built his dark brown wooden house on Lake George. He has artifacts from all over the world. He has traveled a lot and many people have given him gifts. He was an Episcopalian priest.

Grampa

Gramma had two cats: Chaumbey and Murphy. The first one was a Siamese cat and the latter one was a big, fluffy yellow one much like Nancy Marnell's "Puffy". Chaumbey used to hide in the birchwood Nativity. There was a turtle named 'Murtle' too. Karl used to feed the turtle lettuce. The cats did not live long after Gramma died.

Grampa was desolate. He holed himself up in his room with a bottle of Crown Royal. One day, Uncle Cyrus and his wife Margey brought him a

little black poodle for consideration. He did not want any part of that.
Being an old softie, he took "Sukee" and he had a purpose.

The nurses and nurses' aides at the hospital and nursing home all took
Grampa under their wings. He would take his coffee breaks with them.
They were good for him because they would make him laugh and he
would listen to their travails.

It was at this time, that little Virginia took to honing up on her
grandfather. She was not sure how to approach him after Gramma died.
One evening she came down from the lake on her bike. She cold see
Grampa in his living room with his dark glasses on. He wore these as his
eyes had to adjust from the artificial light to the natural daylight as he
worked the night shift. He had the TV on. Virginia went into "20 Carillon"
and sat in the winged chair that used to be one of Aunt Dorcas'. Aunt
Dorcas was Grampa's sister. She had fine taste. Anyway, Virginia
managed, "Hi Grampa," Then, she just sat there - without saying a word.
Grampa sat in his green rocker, the one that Mrs. Greenough had re-
upholstered for him. Tears streamed down Virginia's face. She thought
she had better leave. But in that moment, Grampa and Virginia bonded.
She felt his pain and desolation keenly for the loss of his one true love.
She left.

While a lot of her classmates were interested in partying and dating,
Virginia was only interested in consoling Grampa. Indeed she would visit
folks all over town if there was a death in their family. She would make a
baked good and show up. Perhaps she was a nuisance, or a distraction. It
made her feel good. She still dreamt of being a movie star though.

She would return to Grampa's almost every evening. He continued
Gramma's tradition of having a Schweppes' Ginger ale on hand. Then
one morning when Virginia was at home, Grampa called and told her to
be sure and stop by because he had a pecan pie for her. He bought it at a
local bake sale. When Virginia stopped in that evening, he told her to pick
something out of the corner hutch in which to remember Gramma.
There was a little wooden angel with wings. It was musical, a Hummel. It

played, "When You Wish Upon a Star.........." Virginia walked down Champlain Avenue as this treasure played in her hand - in her head - in her heart -

Mrs. Dechame

Summer went by. Virginia's dear friend Mrs. Dechame invited her out to lunch often. She was an attractive lady; very classy. She took Virginia under her wing. Virginia would see her at the Fort. Mrs. Dechame was instrumental in bringing the Scottish Tattoo to the Fort. Many of the people traveling would be staying at her house. The Audettes always went to the Scottish games and Military Tattoo growing up. Virginia especially loved the bag pipes and the Scottish dances with the swords on the ground. Mrs. Dechame was hosting a big fete at her house after the event. Virginia and her younger sister Mary would serve the punch. There was this crazy man from Canada roaming around. He must have had too much to drink. Then the ice water overflowed from its bucket. An electrical chord was lying in it. Virginia got a shock. That man was not the only one getting a "buzz".

First, the Dechames lived in what Grampa told Virginia was the Colonel Hamilton house. This was set back on the road leading into the Fort. It was a stone house - a real Revolutionary War house. One could imagine a big cauldron hanging over the fireplace. Colonel Hamilton wrote books on the Fort. Then, the Dechames moved. They had this manse built on the Fort Road. The setting was idyllic. It was like a medieval forest. The air was thick with pine. It was on historical ground. The Fort was less than a mile from there. It was a big white mansion with pillars. The rooms were like something out of the Architectural Digest. The furnishings were museum quality. Surely "Spirits" filled the air. Mrs. Dechame was prescient. She was very aware of her surroundings. She could sense things that might yet occur. One night, she got up and there was a Revolutionary War soldier in her kitchen. Mrs. Dechame was natural with such an occurrence. She had a great empathy for all those involved in war. She had impressed upon the young girl the cold, the hunger and the pain that these young men endured for our freedom. She loved Poetry.

One of her ancestors wrote verse. She was particularly fond of a Civil War poet by the name of Reverend Abram Ryan. His poetry is exquisite. Mrs. Dechame gave young Virginia a book of his poetry. Interestingly enough, there is a poem entitled "Virginia" in it. Mrs. Dechame taught Virginia so much about history, literature, travel, food, drink and fashion. Virginia admired her greatly and she tried to emulate her. What better model. Not many know that Our Blessed Mother was invoked by the French at Fort Ticonderoga. Our Lady heard theri Aves amidst the battle cries. She appeared bringing these men to victory. The Blue and White with gold Fleur de Lis was raised in Her Honour!

Along the Fort Road

One occurrence took place on the Fort Road less than a quarter of a mile before Mrs. Dechame's house. The teRieles were living there. They had just gotten a pretty brown horse. Virginia had never been on a horse in her life. She was only about nine and a half years old when Jeanne propped her up on the horse's bareback. The horse must have sensed the child's apprehension. He took off like lightening while Virginia held onto his mane. They went under an apple tree. It was only by the grace of God that the child ducked or she would have been the headless horseman. Her Guardian Angel was by her side. The teRiele's had chickens and farther down the road, near the Ferry Landing Pop teRiele ran the Fort Farm. There were lots of cows there - a real bucolic setting.

Grandfather told Virginia a funny story that also happened at this same house - the old Murray house on the Fort Road. The lady of the house called for Grampa to look at her furnace. This was years before the teRieles moved there. Anyway, the lady stood on the cellar stairs where light shone between the steps. She was wearing only her robe. More than the furnace was visible to the plumber. She always had a fancy for Grandfather.

Virginia's dear friend Christine teRiele would invite Virginia to her house. Jeanne is the older sister who is Annie's age. They were digging one day in the backyard. They found these Indian beads, an old kitchen pot, blue glass bottles, and buttons. Christine's Mom use to casually display them on her kitchen window sill.

The teRieles were jokesters. Mrs. teRiele got a set of that new "unbreakable" Chinet dishes. Jeanne decided to hurl one at Virginia, "Here Virginia, catch!" It was not a frisbee. It smashed into smithereens though it was not supposed to. Then, Christine played a joke on her friend. Her father had just gotten out of the shower. Christine hollared for Virginia to come upstairs. "Where are you?" The child asked. "I am in my parent's room. Come on in." Well, Virginia never lived that one down! Christine's Dutch Dad referred to his daughter's friend as "Sneaky Peek". Practical jokes ran in the family. Mr. teRiele bore a striking resemblance to the late, and great Pope, Saint John Paul II. Virginia had a white hat that she wore to church and when Ted teRiele put it on, one was ready to receive a blessing. Before any blessing, Mr. teRiele would pass the basket at church. He used to enjoy shaking that basket vigorously in front of Virginia when he knew she did not have anything to put in it. One time, there was a lady, Mrs. McCaughin, who lived on a farm just after the intersection heading up the Fort Road. She gave little Virginia a dime to put in the collection. Mr. teRiele or "Dutchy" as he was affectionately called, did have the heart to match His Holiness. He would take Virginia to Stewarts after the Sunday evening Mass with his wife Tillie. They would have strawberry sundaes. If you were joining the teRieles for dinner at their farm, you were sure to have fresh beef and postatoes. You could smell the Tide laundry soap when you walked in theri house. Tillie used Octagon to wash the dishes. Chrissy and Virginia would make crafts, like a pig, out of these bottles when they were empty.

Another quarter of a mile, before the Murray house, the teRieles used to live in another Fort house. It was on the right hand side of the road. It is purported to be haunted. Virginia stayed overnight there several times. She was eating her "cheerios" when Christine told her mother to give Virginia more as there was only one oat left floating around in her bowl. Having a good appetite, the child was delighted. The MacAllisters lived on the other side of this house. They had a soft ice cream stand. They went to St. Mary's same as the teRieles and Audettes did.

Then There Were Twelve

In February of 1978, Mother had her eighth girl and twelvth child - Sarah Dorcas Stephanie. There was an eleven year gap between the then youngest Tisdale. It was very exciting having a new baby in the home. Sometimes Tillie teRiele babysat for her. They called her "Sarah Cupcake".

Family 1979

Close Calls

There was a family renting the Forcier camp off of Black Point Road, not far from the Boat Launch. Virginia was invited up for the afternoon to join Rosa and Christine for a picnic. Rosa was a beautiful and very popular girl. They all went swimming. What strange thoughts that get in a child's head. Virginia used to imagine that she could fly from one stump to the next in front of her house. Now there was a small cliff. Virginia was seized with this desire to jump or dive off of it - neither of which she knew how to do. In fact, she did not know how to swim. Thank God this was not executed. It was shallow below. Rosa was very sensitive to Virginia's feelings. Christine was going to sleep over and Rosa did not want Virginia to feel left out because she could only have one guest. She explained this very tactfully. Virginia always appreciated Rosa's sensitivity.

On another occasion, Virginia was with Jelissa Wilson, whom she babysat for, at the Roger's Rock Club at the end of Baldwin Road. Jelissa's family summered at the Rookery. Virginia spent a fair amount of time there as a companion to old Mrs. Wilson. Now the 'Rookery' is in Virginia's family. Her aunt and uncle own it. Virginia has always liked it there. However, there is a resident black snake. He takes care of the mice. Virginia's sister Jane named him 'Chester' after the manservant of the same name. Well, one day Virginia and Jelissa were swimming in front of the little building known as the casino. Virginia managed to get stuck under a dock. She was submerged and there were catfish all around her. She starting praying, "Hail Mary, Full of Grace......" At once, she was in a clearing.

Again, in the waters of Lake George, but this time at the Ticonderoga Beach - on the far side where the Boys' Camp youngsters used to go, Virginia nearly drowned. There are these rocks straight out. Christine and some other classmates were going to swim out to them. "Come on, let's go!" They shouted. Virginia gave in to peer pressure. The water was rough and it was over her head. She feigned the "dog paddle" but she really did not know how to swim. It was by the grace of God that she made it unscathed. Well, almost unscathed. Christine wanted to celebrate Virginia's birthday. She had just turned the legal, for that time, age of eighteen. When they were on shore, she produced a bottle of whiskey and a bottle of 7-Up. It seemed impolite to refuse. She had never had alcohol before. She fell violently ill. Her room was spinning. It was awful and it really put the young girl off the drink.

Daddy would give his children a bottle of champagne for their eighteenth birthday - a rite of passage. Grampa gave Virginia a taste of Amaretto, a lady's drink. It was hard to get down. Moderation is key - in all things. Fahter Salmon told the class in Catechism that if one has too much steak, he finds himself tiring of it.

Father Salmon

Father Salmon was an influential figure in young Virginia's life. He was a formidable presence much like John Wayne. He actually resembled John Wayne. John Wayne was one of Virginia's heroes too. She wrote to him as a teenager telling him how she wanted to be a movie star. he replied with a handwritten autograph on a black and white stock photo from the movie 'True Grit'. He wrote, "Good Luck Virginia, John Wayne".

One Sunday evening Mass, Virginia's good friend Christine and Virginia were the lectors. Well, Christine did the Readings, and Virginia did the Prayers of the Faithful. There were instructions taped to the podium. Virginia proceded to read the instructions, "Please be sure to read at every Mass..............." when she suddenly realized her foible. She broke out in nervous laughte. Chrissy got laughing too. Father took it in stride.

Father Salmon had a loud, booming voice. He also had a nice singing voice. He was known for singing "God Bless America" at the end of every Mass. This had special meaning to him. Not only was Father a great American who served his country in the foreign wars, but, he knew the great Kate Smith who made this song famous. Kate Smith converted to Catholicism. It was Father Salmon who baptized her. Kate Smith lived in Lake Placid which was not that far from Ticonderoga.

Father wore a black Persian fur Ambassador's hat. His favorite singer was the Irish tenor John McCormack. Father was a traditionalist. He was also ahead of his times. He could see the way the world was going. He would go to the missions in Vianna, Brazil raising money to help the poor people there. He was devoted to his mother. Will never forget when his mother died and he told how he had given her some ambrosia just beforehand. Father was from Brooklyn. When he was young, he earned money as an usher in a theater. He got to see lots of movies this way. His family were big in the Bell Telephone Company. Father had a quick wit and a good sense of humor. He used to take us kids roller skating in Glens Falls. He was a man's man and fearless in the face of justice. He impressed upon Virginia the value of the sanctity of life. He guided her and helped her as a spiritual father. For that, she is forever grateful. He was a "Faith of Our Fathers" man at a time when the "Kumbaya" crowd were moving in. Some people were intimidated by him and they wrote to the bishop to have him removed. Father was prudent, cautious, and quiet. They missed out.

Godmother

Virginia became a Godmother in her senior year. A sweet childhood friend had asked her to be a Godmother for her just as sweet daughter Dawn Marie. Father Salmon Baptized the baby.

Up With People

One evening when Virginia was a senior in high school, she was babysitting for Hal and Beverly Otley's children on First Street (Algonkin Street). The Mill had sponsored a concert that was performing at the high school. It was an international, inspirational, happy-go-lucky group singing and dancing. The first thing that Mr. Otley said when he got home was, "I can see you in this group Virginia." She had never seen them or heard of them but that was enough for her to inquire about them. The group was called "Up With People". Virginia wrote letters and sent inquiries out. She applied and interviewed with a staff member in Burlington, Vermont. She was very excited when she received a letter of acceptance. Though she would have to take off ten pounds due to the lighting. Mrs. Curtis from Weight Watchers called and offered her free membership. She also had to have a physical which included a certain exam the likes of which she had never had. Doctor Tom in his wisdom spared her of this trauma and simply signed the form to her great relief. Now she had to raise $5,000. It was a lot, but the whole town rallied around her.

For all the running that Virginia did in high school for the Track team, she had hoped to get a "Letter" - that is, the "Letter 'T'" which could then be appliqued to a sweater or a jacket. She ran the two-mile and over six miles every day in training. However, she never received one. Surely it was an oversight, but it was a disappointment just the same.

Something that bothered Virginia terribly in school was when one girl in gym class was made to stand in the corner for forgetting her gym clothes. The girl was from a poor family and she was introverted. The gym teacher would holler at her mercilessly. This happened more than once.

Virginia finished her senior year. She was not sure if she would graduate. One of her teachers, or perhaps a couple, she sensed, did not like her. She was a little bit too enthusiastic for their liking - too much "Mary Sunshine". She secretly feared that one of them might not pass her on her Regents exam. That did not transpire. Virginia and Henry were handed their diplomas by theri mother. It was a tradition at the time, that a teacher who was a parent of the graduate could present his graduating son or daughter with the diploma. It rained that day so the Commencement Exercises were held in the school auditorium that day. Virginia was filled with emotion.

Summertime

Virginia was riding her bike down from the lake one July day when she stopped at her grandfather's. She asked her grandfather if she could move in with him. She thought it would be neat to have her own room. He wanted her to be respectful of her parents so he admonished her to ask them. Virginia's father was in the hospital at the time. He had throat Cancer. He had this megaphone which he would talk into. He had stopped smoking "cold turkey". He acquiesced. Grampa would tell everyone that Little Virginia would ride her bike bringing a little bit of her stuff with her each time she came. He seemed to get a kick out of it. It filled a void for him.

Virginia continued to work at the Fort that summer. Before the season ended, she went to work at a gas station on the top of Wicker Hill. She could work more hours and save for the group she intended to join. She also planned a bazaar in the early Fall. Father Salmon permitted her to use the school gym. This tall, gorgeous blonde lady came to the gas station. Her name was Nancy Marnell. She donated lots of things for Virginia's bazaar. Nancy was married to Virginia's second cousin. They had two sons who are cousins once removed or something like that.

August of 1977

In August of 1977, Virginia's cousin was killed in a car accident. She was Mother's first cousin though she was the same age as Virginia's younger sister Mary. God rest Michelle.

The Good Doctor

Virginia was still coming up short with the necessary funds. One of the nurses from the hospital who worked when Grampa worked, suggested that she approach Dr. Tom. Virginia never would have thought of that. She did write him a letter explaining what she wanted to do. A couple of days later, a check arrived in the mail for a thousand dollars. Virginia has that in her scrap book. The best part, was the letter that accompanied it. He was making light of his magnanimity. Virginia was candystriping at the hospital the next day and upon seeing the good doctor, she ran up to him, and embraced him - thanking him. This probably embarrassed him as he was very low-key. Father Salmon was looking on smiling.

Trials and Tribulation

As much as Virginia was floating on air, her wisdom teeth were impacted. They had to come out. It was done in two sessions. Virginia felt like Steve

Lawrence with her bulging cheeks. They were so swollen and she was in so much pain. She could not eat so she was definitely losing the required weight. Dr. McHugh is to be credited for his expertise. He cleaned out what had gotten infected. She was put on anti-biotics. It was a couple of weeks before she was feeling better.

Added to this bit of pain, Grampa and Virginia's mother and father were making trips over to the hospital in Burlington. Uncle Cyrus was in the ICU. He had cirrhosis of the liver. He was dying. Virginia went over to visit him too. A helmet was on his head. It was both shocking and upsetting. The last week of September in 1978, Uncle Cyrus joined his mother. Grampa was inconsolable. Virginia was crushed. He is buried on the top of Chilson Hill - on one of the "Three Brothers' Mountains". In the Valley below, his mother is laid to rest. The family Cross is engraved with "I will lift mine eyes, unto the hills, whence cometh my Help....."

Little Virginia was in the habit of attending funerals. She would don her black hat, wear a nice dress, put on gloves and she always had a handkerchief in her purse. She would lose herself in the details. She was not the disposable type. She should have been complimented, but her pride got in the way when one day while the church bells were pealing, Virginia made her way into St.Mary's, Mrs. Connery exclaimed , "A Lady is born!" Had not she always been a lady or was she like a handkerchief girl. Didn't her grandfather tell her that he had one goal in life for her, and that was, to be a lady.

Virginia spoke in front of the Kiwanis Club about her project still trying to garner funds. There was a luncheon at Eddie's Restaurant on the Hague Road - not far from Tuffertown where one of her aunts and uncles lived. Grampa was waiting in the bar. He decided to buy this one man, Mr. Wilton a drink. This same man owned a lumber store. Virginia had approached him as a potential donor. He was also the president of this local organization. While he refused the young girl at his store, he was now shaking hands with her while presenting a check to her on behalf of this organization. Grandfather, in the meantime, took the liberty to tell him, "You cheap bastard, you could not give my granddaughter a five dollar donation from your store and now you are going to get credit here." The next thing, the cameras are clicking away for the local newspapers as Mr. Wilton presents Virginia a check albeit gritting his teeth.

Grampa derived great satisfaction out of putting people in their place. He said that Gramma was better at it. She did it in a nice way.

with God at Our Side

That Thanksgiving, Aunt Karlene invited her father and Virginia for dinner. She and Uncle Datus lived near Plattsburgh, New York. It was strange for Virginia not to be having it at 303 where she grew up. Aunt Karlene does things very nicely. She had little boxes of Russell Stover chocolates at each setting. As they were leaving, the firs snowfall of the season was in the air. Grampa did most of the driving coming home. It was slow going as lots of cars had slid off the road. Grampa was getting tired. Virginia took the wheel and drove very gingerly. They were coming up Convent Hill in Port Henry when horror of horrors - a huge semi truck was coming down the hill around a bend. Something extraordinary happened. Grampa's vehicle went up the hill in the left lane, and miraculously, the big tractor trailer truck came down in the right lane, which should have been their lane. They narrowly missed a collision. Grampa and Virginia were silent. Virginia continued driving in disbelief. A few days went by before either of them broached the subject. They had to confirm it with each other to make sure neither had imagined that.

In just over one month, Virginia would embark on a new adventure in the New Year. Mrs. Dechame had given her a wardrobe rewarding her for taking off the required weight. She put the French brown tweed skirt and matching jacket that had leather piping trim on it. She braided her hair like her Gramma Audette did - only she wore them like a headband regally. She topped her outfit off with a woolen cap. Grandfather and mother drove her to the Albany Airport. They got a bite to eat in the restaurant there. Virginia could not eat. She felt a pit in her stomach. Shortly, they had their farewells. They were all trying to hold back tears as little Virginia boarded the aircraft to Tallahassee. She would have a change at JFK airport. This was her first time on an airplane and a window seat at that! How about that Lizzy! Little sister is on her way!

PART II

Away She Goes

I had to switch airplanes in New York. I did not realize that there was a bus shuttle that would take one to the corresponding departure gate. I went outside and walked quite a distance before finding the Eastern Airline terminal. As I entered this part of the airport, this young woman approached me. She was a follower of Reverend Moon - otherwise known as a "Moonie". I had heard of them but I did not know much more than that. She is touching my braids and asking me for money. I told her I only have Travelers Checks. She offered to help me cash them, but I fled from her. My eyes were opening up. I went upstairs in the terminal and soon was able to board my plane.   Upon getting situated, I asked the airline stewardess, "Mam, is there a bathroom on the airplane?" To which she replied yes. I passed this young lady sitting down who must have thought I was weird as I made my way to the restroom.

There was gingerale and peanuts for the first leg of the trip. We were served a light dinner on the flight to Tallahassee. I was saving the napkin from the airplane, the in-flight magazine, the plastic cup with the logo on it. This was all new to me. We got in quite late to Tallahassee. One of the directors met me at the airport. That same girl who heard me ask about the bathroom was there too. It seems she was going to be part of the same traveling group as I. There was another gal from Tennessee who came in on a different flight. Her name was Laura. She reminded me of my brother Henry. She had short brown hair and these brown eyes like Henry's. We were to be put up in a hotel that night. Tk, one of the staff, drove us to The Days Inn. No one wanted to room with me so I was on my own. That other girl had a thick Northern Irish accent. Her name was Patricia and she was from Belfast. She and Laura shared one room and I had one a couple of doors down the corridor. This was my first time on my own. There was this coin apparatus beside the bed. You could put a quarter in it and get a massage. Naturally, I had to try it out. I called Grampa on the phone beside the bed. He was very happy to hear that I had arrived safely to my destination.

Training in North Florida

The next morning, we had breakfast at a nearby Denny's. Then, T.K., (Tom Klass), drove us to the campus of North Florida Junior College in Madison. We were given our practice schedules. Introductions were made. We listened to current events and were briefed on protocol and such. We had lunch in the cafeteria - black-eyed peas and chicken and jello. We then were allocated with our host families. I would be rooming with another girl. Her name was Jacinta, named after one of the visionaries from Fatima, Portugal. There were no other similarities. We were staying with a family by the name of Jackson. The host father worked on ships - and traveled all over. The host mother was a maternal, stay-at home mom. There was an older son and daughter who lived with them. They were very nice or so they seemed. Jacinta presented two Waterford crystal glasses as a host gift. I was not prepared as I had to borrow half of my tuition from the bank to get the necessary funds to join Up With People. She tried to shame me because i did not have a gift for them. I thought, my goodness, we will be staying with more than a hundred families throughout the year, it will be difficult to have gifts for them all. Of course, initially, we will be one month while we are in training with this family. I thought, there is something that I do have. I brought Sloan Wilson's latest book with me. He was a renown author who lived in Ticonderoga. He wrote "The Man in The Grey Flannel Suit" and "A

Summer Place" and his latest novel was "Small Town". I presented this to my hosts. Mr. Jackson later criticized me saying that I had no business reading such a book and that is was " kind of raw" for a young lady to be reading. I felt embarrassed and humiliated. It seems I was being held up against Jacinta. Mr. Jackson would compare us out in public and extol Jacinta and for some reason, he would put me down. I was uncomfortable staying there. I was in my bathrobe at the breakfast table and he turned that around as though I were being inappropriate. I could not do right by him no matter what. Yet I was begging to get to church that first Sunday as I had never missed Mass in my life. Jacinta proceded to tell me that I was selfish for wanting to go to church as it was muddy out as a result of a lot of rain.   We did go the following week however, only it was to a Baptist Church. The third week we did make it, to my consolation, to a Catholic church.

If I was not uncomfortable on this homefront, I was a little with the group as we began our rigorous training. They were long days of exercising, singing, learning routines and testing to see where we would best fit in. I had always thought that I wanted to be a movie star, but in this group that is wholesome for all intents and purposes, I was getting turned off by the ones who were so full of themselves who practically insisted on being up front or the stars of the show. It is interesting to watch human nature in action. I saw the whole gamut here. Well, there were over one hundred of us in Cast E and we were thrust together to create this great, international, "I get a kick out of life"- type show. There was also, a tremendous amount of talent in our midst. People come from all walks of life and this is what made it unique as we joined forces and put our best foot forward producing a dyanmite two hour show.

There was one fellow from Louisianna, his name was Jude. He was my Square Dance partner, and he grew increasingly annoyed with me. I would be beat off or something and he wanted instant perfection. He seemed to be smitten with this gal from Mississippi. Her name was Beverly. She was absolutely stunning to look at. Indeed she was Miss Mississippi. Jude would pray with Beverly I noticed. Come to find out,

Jude lost his mother when he was an infant. I felt sorry for him, but he was still a pain to be around. I seemed to gravitate towards that Irish girl Patricia from Belfast. Only I had to ask her to repeat everything because I was unaccustomed to her accent. We would sit together for lunch. There was also this very affable fellow from Monroe, Connecticut. His name was Mark Day. He was a lot of fun to be around. I would return my tray to the dishwasher station and this heavyset young man would say "Thank you". I would reply, "You are welcome." What I didn't realize, was that, by merely being polite, something this fellow was unaccustomed to, he was daily growing a crush on me. His name was Ira. He would write me these letters on paper torn out of a notebook in pencil. It was getting uncomfortable no matter where I went!

Feeling Homesick

I would call Grampa every week or he would call me and then he would write letters to encourage me. One letter was particularly upsetting as it concerned my oldest brother Georgie. He had to go to Boston to have this tumor in his mouth removed. I stayed in my room that night and Jacinta laid me out in lavender for not being polite spending time with the hosts. then I told her that I was preoccupied and when I told her about my brother, she backed down. I believe she was from Galway.

Our show was finally coming together. We had been given our show costumes. Mine was a fitted white dress trimmed in Royal blue. It had a couple of blue-trimmed slits on the front. It was a shimmery satiny material. We had white showpants for underneath. Some of the girls in the cast were outfitted with the same style dress with the square neck trimmed in the same blue, only their dresses were orange colored. The fellows all wore Royal blue colored pants and tops with white trimmed collars. We traipsed across a field with the stage set-up blocks and had our Cast photo taken. It was a cold January day too. We were also given an outfit for our assemblies and acoustic mini-shows. For the ladies, it was khaki slacks and a striped shirt. Oh how I love stripes! This one had sort of olive, black and white stripes. Then, after weeks of stretching and exercising; practicing and memorizing songs and learning dance steps;

setting up and striking the stage equipment the day arrived in February of 1979 for our first show. Only, I would not be in it. I would not miss it for anything except I had incapaciting menstrual cramps. I really don't think I was missed, except perhaps by Ira, the dishwasher. The Jacksons all came back that evening with glowing reports of how good their Irish lassie was. They had no concern for how I was. I did manage to make it to the Saturday concert. I donned the "Pancake number 2" make up as required and it was rather satisfying being on stage after working so hard to put the show together. The most fun part was doing "La Bamba" Congo line where we would go right out in the audience and get folks to join in the line. Also, during our staging in Madison, we had great, inspirational speakers who would visit us. There was Mr. Blatant Belk sharing his vision and the history of Up With People. Mr. King Cole told how he renovated Spokane, Washington for the Expol Dale Penny gave an exegesis on the financial status of UWP. Mrs. Virginia Trevitt inspired us all reminding us, "You are all leaders....." There were other fine speakers. We were even inspired by a timely presentation of another cast - Cast D when we still had another rigorous week to go before showtime. Our group was weary so this was a welcome boost.

Virginia

The Show and Tour Begin

One of my favorite things we did was going out to perform in schools nursing homes, schools for the blind or mentally handicapped. The response was most palpable. Thus on February 12th we sang on the steps of Madison City Hall as the Mayor read a proclamtion. We sang one last time for Madison and then boarded the buses going on the road - up the Eastern Seaboard to over ninety different families - to different countries, and to different cultures.

One fellow in the group was Jim from Texas. He used to carry his satellite radio around with him wherever he went. He would listen to Rush Limbaugh. I got a kick out of him. His personality reminded me of my brother Karl's.

There was a gal from St. Thomas, US Virgin Islands. I think she represented that territory in a beauty pageant. Her name was Wanda. She had this exotic look to her. She looked like she should be advertising Bali bras. She was a little bit older, maybe 26 while the median age of the cast member was 19.   We enjoyed each other's company. I will never forget how she waxed her legs when we roomed together with a host family in Palma de Mallorca. I had never heard of that. Wanda had quite a style and she could really pull it off. Her parents were from India originally . Wanda had dark skin and dark almond shaped eyes. She had perfect diction and she spoke several languages.

There were some cliques in the group. There were a few who always had to get on their soap boxes and enlighten the rest of us. Then there were the ones that might be short-tempered with you while they would pray together before a show. This always struck me funny. There were some who made fun of others but today they are holier than thou.

We had to set up and strike all the stage equipment, sound system and lighting before and after each city we staged in. From Madison, Florida we went to Perry, Florida and then to the poultry capital inLive Oak. Then we made our way to Dothan, Alabama with a stop at Sunnyland Meat Packing Plant. Then is was onto Valdosta, Georgia. The truck with all the equipment in it broke down. We did a show or an "Assembly" - a shortened version of our actual show at Georgia Sheriff's Boys Ranch.

February 25th brought us to Cairo, Georgia having been greeted by the student council, fire truck and police escort. We did a high school assembly; had pot luck dinner with the student council, band and chorus. We had a sell out show that evening.

Virginia and castmate Diane - Spring, 1979

Host Families

One of my host mothers, had a pecan tree in front of her humble little house. She gave me a whole box of them. I am humbled when I think on this as she was a poor widow. God love her. We had our share of pecan pie in the South along with grits, black eyed peas and fried chicken. I remember Grampa calling me up one time to say he had a pecan pie for me and to stop on my way down from the lake to pick it up.

One free day in Georgia took us to the beautiful Callaway Gardens in Pine Montain. We were all given bikes to ride. It was such a nice day.

One thing I enjoyed, that was a novelty to me, was the Shoney's restaurants down South. They had these wonderful strawberry pies with mounds of whipped cream on them. Some of my hostfamilies would take me there after a show or for dinner.

Flood

We ended up with two free days in Pensacola as it rained like crazy. There was severe flooding and one of our cast members had to be rescued with a boat from where she was staying. We did a show at the Sacred heart Hospital and two mall shows on floating stages. Pensacola was a fun place for me. I stayed with a lady whose husband never returned from Vietnam. She had a daughter. They took me to the Jazz district which could be likened to New Orleans. The Old Opera Theatre was of great interest too - reportedly haunted.

Next stop on the tour was Panama City where Miss Watermelon greeted us. My host family had cockroaches as I recall. Not uncommon in that hot climate. We did our show at the civic center. TWo days later we returned to Pensacola for a sell-out show in that flooded theater.

What Color Is God's Skin

One of Up With People's signature songs, besides "Up, Up With People" is "What Color is God's Skin". This is very beautiful and transcends all racial barriers. This was the aim of the founder of this group - one Mr. Blatant J. Belk. He was concerned about the direction of the young people during the turbulent 1960's. This was his idea and a very good one at that.

Then it was onto Selma, Alabama where Dr. F.D. Reese, a Civil Rights Movement leader with Dr. Martin Luther King, spoke to us. We had an "Acoustic" at a mental Health Transitional Home, Good Samaritan Nursing Home, and Warren Manor Nursing Home as well as at the National Guard Armory.

March 9th - We traveled to Auburn with a stop-over in Montgomery to perform for the Governor of Alabama. We did Assemblies for Drake and Boykin Middle Schools. There was free time for us at Auburn University followed by a show for Village Mall ending with another show in Sports Arena. I stayed with a family by the name of Ferris. This intrigued me as this is my paternal grandmother's name. They were a lovely family with three fine-looking sons. They had a stately home.

Tuskegee, Alabama ws next on the agenda with a performance for Veterans Hospital. Mr. A.P. Torrence, the vice-president of Tuskegee University was a featured speaker along with Mayor Johnny Ford. We did a high school assembly, a tour of george Washington Carver Museum and Booker T. Washington's Home. We did an Acoustic for Tuskegee Laboratory and Learning Center and another one at Magnolia Nursing Home. We had an Irish dinner in this town and also a pot luck with our host families. Moreover, I had the best baked beans I have ever had in my life with my host family here. I was with an African American family. The head of the family told me that he puts mustard, onions, sausage, and molasses in his beans. Boy were they tasty!

Down South

Thus the show and the brimming tour continued with a different variation in each town or city. In Scottsboro, Alabama a lady was hit by a falling light. There would be other incidents too - technical problems where we might have had to mingle with the crowd to compensate.

One time, after rehearsal, everyone was getting dressed for the show. It seems Jacinta could not find her show pants. Suddenly, mine turned up missing. Robin H. was in tune to this. she is a petite little girl but she can hold her own. She went and retrieved this part of my costume for me. Some in the cast were protective of me, like Robin and Dana was too.

We disco danced with the senior citizens in Huntsville, made the evening News and the Today Show. We visited the Nasa Space and Rocket Center and Museum. We attended a golf seminar. Speaking of golf, our next stop was Hilton Head, South Carolina. I saw Herbie Green walking with his family and we greeted each other. I remember we had lunch in Atlanta and the buses got lost on the way. The Heritage Golf Classic was taking place. We had a cookout. We also were treated to bike rides in this beautiful park. We were also making a tape for the Braves Game. My Aunt Jane loves the Braves.

After Hilton Head, the next high-falluting place was to the International Polo Tournament in West Palm Springs. We had a show at the Fountainbleau Hotel on Miami Beach and later one that night with Pat and Debbie Boone. The protocol was pretty strict. My host family here had just survived an awful tragedy. The man of the house had been murdered. I just came across a Christmas card that the family had sent me.

After Hollywood, Florida, it was to the Southernmost point in the United States - Ernest Hemingway's Key West, Florida. This is where I was introduced to Key Lime Pie. I just made some the other day. I also had my first taste of Grouper fish here. I love that fish! We got a tram tour of the island and we continuued taping for the Braves game. Kevin and Dave gave us a Karate demonstration. Later we had a high school assembly.

In Miami we had lunch on the beach, learned the National Anthem for the Braves game, had a talk from the vice president of UWP, Mr. Wisher. Then half of the cast performed in Hobe Sound for a private affair. I was not in that half.

Georgia and The Carolinas

Then there was a long bus ride to Monroe, Georgia where one of our cast members is from - Cathy Connell. Cathy is a lovely, sweet girl. She was always kind to me. She was also very popular in her hometown. Here, we had a pre-game show for the Braves opening season. Cincinnati Reds vs. Atlanta Braves. We had free time in Atlanta. Our concert brought more than 38,000 people not counting tv coverage.

Burlington, North Carolina - an acoustic at Smith Elementary school along with a host of other schools. A tour of Carolina Biological Supply co.; an acoustic at a Drug Abuse Center. We had our founder's sister, Mrs. Jane Moncure speak. We had a Passover Supper.

April 13th, New Bern, North Carolina - this is the place where Pepsi was invented. Mayor Morgan proclaimed UWP Week upon our arrival. The usual Acoustics and Assemblies at the various schools were in order. We then had a tour of the Hattaras Yachts where we saw how they were made. That was fascinating. We also visited Camp Le Jeune - the world's largest amphibios Marine Training Base. I was right at home since my brother Thomas and I used to play in those tanks behind the Armory in my hometown. One of the public relations staff, Steve Schmader, was given a Porsche to drive as his P.R. car. I was here for Easter. My host mother made these fabulous chocolate peanut butter Easter eggs. They are a closely guarded secret recipe. Her husband is a Marine. They had a great rapport I noticed. They were constantly exchanging witticisms back and forth and laughing. They had two little children. We went to Easter Services in this pretty white church that reminded me of our Community building back home. The music was uplifting and while it was all very nice, I was missing the Easter Vigil that I was accustomed to growing up. Afterward, we had a delicious Easter brunch and I had one of those prized Easter eggs!

The latter part of the month brought us to Goldsboro, and Greensboro, North Carolina. We visited A & T University, Gilford College and then toured the R.J. Reynolds Tobacco Company in Winston-Salem. Mark Day and I pretended that we were smoking cigarettes. Though they were very strict there about touching any tobacco debris that may have fallen on the floor. Greensboro is also the place where I had my first taste of Divinity fudge. Four other girls in the group were rooming with me at this lady's house. She made all this fudge. I will never forget that Divinity fudge. Speaking of Divinity - she gave me a little prayer book and Christian pin.

Some of the most memorable and fun times I had in my Up With People year took place in our "Green Room". This was a fifteen minute or so time frame set aside before we went on stage to get revved up for our show. Different cast mates would perform, do skits, charades, any antics, or sing, share an experience - it could be anything. It was a free for all. It was where we were our true selves and we shared that amongst our peers. Wanda and I partook in a green room. She sang "People" (who need people... etc." and I did a dance to it. I remember Jeff H. thought it was a bit heavy, if not heartfelt, right before the show. In the spirit of UWP, I partook a couple of times - usually met with consternation.

In Gastonia, North Carolina, we had a career day. My room mate Beth, who was also the cast nurse, chose a chiropractor. It only seemed natural for me to select the local ice cream parlor. Bresler's Ice Cream. The manager showed me how to make an ice cream cake with a doll. Her skirt was the ice cream cake. Then he got pizza for our lunch. It was a lot of fun. As I was walking in the mall later that day, I ran into Patricia Murphy and Steve Schmader. A man with Culligan Water wanted us to pose next to the non-stop water spout that seemed to be floating in mid-air. There were so many new things to see and do and my eyes were always opening up to it. Thank you Lord for this experience.

After Gastonia, North Carolina, it was onto West Virginia and then to Winchester, Virginia. We visited Harper's Ferry. We were there for the Shenandoah Apple Blossom Festival. The grand feature, was the parade. Jimmy Dean was the Grand Marshall. It is the second largest in the world. Later, we did an Acoustic for thirty blind students which was very special. We were in the beautiful Blue Ridge Mountains. Richard Paul and Marie Ferrier were in our audience that night. They are evidently some sort of celebrities.

Beantown

Now we were really heading East to Boston. That was May 6th, 1979. We traveled through eight states to get there. We stopped in New York City. We went to Radio City Music Hall which always reminds me of Betty Wilson as she used to dance as a "Rockette" there. Betty of course lived in Ticonderoga and she gave me free dance lessons. In exchange, I helped babysit for her daughter. Terry Stark and I took the elevator to the top of the World Trade Center. I treasure that picture.

In Boston we performed at many high schools and elementary schools; Perkins School for the Blind; Beth Israel Hospital, Childrens Hospital, Falkner hospital, Ellen James Nursing Home, Home for Little Wanderes,

Marion Manor nursing Home; and Northeastern University. We also performed at Faneuil Hall. It seems The Boston Globe captured us in action with "herself" on the cover. My brother Karl, who was working at the Comptroller's Office in Albany at the time happened to be sipping his morning coffee when he opened the paper. To his astonishment, he saw his sister on the front page - they both shared coffee!

Patricia and I were room mates in Boston. We stayed in one of the suburbs in a beautiful house with a lot of oak and Oriental rugs, grandfather clock, etc. The man of the house was a professor at Boston University. The lady worked outside the home too. She was a great one for leaving notes around the house. "Hang up towels." "Wipe up if something spills" and so on to the point that Patricia and I felt like we were walking on egg shells. We were a little paranoid and we would break out in hysterics over the least thing. It seems there was a statue and as fate would have it, it fell or got knocked off the marble top table. Horror of Horrors! We were trying to remedy the situation. We went out to get glue before it could be detected. Anyway that old "company and fish rule" certainly was applicable for them with us. We never really saw them though. I mean, we left in the morning and returned in the evening. Then they got tickets for our final show which was in the Hynes Auditorium. We kind of ended on a good note. Mark Day and I went to the Boston Pops concert twice. We were given complimentary tickets. We would pretend that we had a box office seat and talk with "sophisticated" accents having Tea during the intermission. Mark bought me a little tin of citrus pastelles there. I still have that tin albeit empty. It is a pretty tin with a Florentine design on it. I also went to a couple of Boston Red Sox games. There again I got complimentary tickets. Mark went with me one day and Larry Swenson the other. I had hot dogs and ice cream both times. This is Grampa's favorite team. A couple of the players came to my hometown when I was growing up. The Knight of Columbus got them to come. Carl Yasztremski was one who came. Henry and Thomas got their autographs. Boston is a great city. We got to tour the Boston Museum of Fine Ats, visit New England Auarium, go on a Grayline busTour, atten a Chamber of Commerce dinner and be featured on WCVB TV - "Good Day Show". We did the Sky Walk of Prudential Center. We had a tour of Symphony Hall, dinner at Northeastern University. We had a speaker from Sidney Farber Cancer Foundation.

Mrs. Dechame had sent me a large parcel of beautiful dresses when I was in Boston. It was a lovely surprise. God Bless her!

We also toured Plymouth, Massachusetts on the way to Provincetown. We had an Acoustic at Truro Central School and a High School Assembly. Trying to think what "Sun Days Parade " was but it was on the itinerary.

Perhaps the ultimate highlight for me during this year was in Provincetown. Grampa drove there to see the show. T.K. (Tom Klass) pulled him out of the audience for the number "Its a Memorable Tune". It was so special the way he included Grampa. Grampa was beaming watching our show. Frank McCarthy admired Grampa's style. He had that straw hat on with the grosgrain ribbon, his vest and pipe. He really had panache. I got to stay with him when he was in town. We had blueberry pancakes for breakfast at the Inn where we stayed. We also walked along the wharf. We were looking for the book "Heidi". It was rather funny as we entered a bookshop that had anything but the book "Heidi" in there. Embarrassedly, we exited and we spotted an artist on the pier. Her name was Beth Moore. She was a college student and I suppose she supplemented her tuition by drawing charcoals of tourists and such. Grampa and I decided to have a go of it. She did both of our profiles in about an half hour. Grampa got the drawing professionally framed. It has become a cherished work of art that captured something unique and special that Grampa and I shared. Thank you Lord for giving me Grampa.

May 20th, 1979 - New Bedford, Massachusetts. We did the routine school acoustics and assemblies. We had a Mr. Andrews come in as a speaker. He spoke on Alcoholism. Then we had a New England dinner with 30 Boy Scouts. We ahd a chorus group patterned after UWP for Green Room that night. It was great.

May 22nd brought us to Worcester or "Wista" as my Aunt Betty likes to say. This is the second largest city in New England. We had a community involvement day, went to Mechanic's Hall and sang at a McDonald's. Had Acoustics at the University of Massachusetts Medical Center for Children and terminally ill patients. Reception in Washburn Hall. A Mr. Porter from the Lions Club spoke for the Sight Foundation. This city is where Cast E was given the official announcement of our upcoming Spanish Tour.

Maryland

May 25th - we traveled to Chestertown, Maryland. We visited the US Naval Academy in Annapolis. The UWP staff put on a surprise show. This is also where one of the naval cadets had asked me to go to the Cotilion. I did not have a proper evening dress so I respectfully declined. But I have often wondered

May 28th - Woodbury, New Jersey. We toured the Philadelphia, Pennsylvania and the General Electric Aerospace center in Valley Forge. Martina talked to us about Spain. WE had shows at Glssboro State College and the Cerebral Palsy Center. I remember my host family. The lady wrote Poetry.

Did Someone Say 'Virginia'

May 31st - Middleburg, Virginia   We performed a private show at the Foxcroft School for Mr. Langhorne Washburn, a member of the Advisory Board of UWP. We had Spanish classes and one of the staff, Sherry Abraham was reassigned to a differnt cast. She was very good. I liked her.

June 1st - Salisbury, Maryland We arrived just in time for the 32nd Annual Delmarva Chicken Festival made in the Worlds largest frying pan. Chicken, chicken and more chicken! The staff were also "roasted".

On June 4th, we had a travel day to Millville by ferry.

On June 7th, we traveled to Bernardsville. We had a picnic and pool party at Tommy Dorsey's estate. We had an Acoustic at A, T & T Telephone Company. Rebecca and Helena who hail form Mexico put on a Spanish dinner. We had a tour of NYC and a free day in town. Our show was at Matheny School (Cerebral Palsy).

Next stop was Manassis, Virginia. This was one of my favorite host families. There were five girls and they would remind one of "Little Women". The family was very sweet. We had a tour of Washington, DC and we did a show with "The Lettermen" at the National Federation of Independent Business Mens Convention. We did another show at the OIC - (Opportunities Industrialization Center). Tony left to travel with another cast. Tony was one of the staff. He was from California - he would make you think of Tony Orlando. We visited Hay Market.

June 15th we were walking on Atlantic City's Boardwalk. I remember seeing these machines in the windows that had all these coins that were just waiting to spill out. We did a show at Holy Spirit High School.

I must have been in the cast that had free time, as Patricia, Mark and I took to the Capital. Half of the cast did a show for the Armed Forces Communication Association at Sheraton Park in Washington, DC.

Michigan

June 20th we made our way to Lansing, Michigan where one of our cast members (Tracy H.) is from. We did shows at teh 4-H Convention at Michigan State University. I picked up a little pink mirror with Shirley Temple's picture on it here. It was like a big Fair going on and there were many booths and stands with all kinds of things. I thought this was an antique until Kevin Hall, one of the staff choreographers informed me, that they only put one out, and after I leave, another one goes out on display.

Wisconsin

Then we moved onto Frank Birr's home city of Two Rivers, Wisconsin. Frank has a young Abraham LIncoln look to him. He is from a large family. I always liked him - maybe because we come from similar backgrounds. We entered the city on fire trucks and even though it was June 23rd, it was very cold out. We had an acoustics for St.Mary's Home for the Aged, Parklawn, Shady Lane, Hamilton Memroial Nursing Home; Two River Day Care Center. WE had our evaluation of the first semester with T.K. We had an International Potluck with hosts, followed by a business seminar. We also had dinner with the senior citizens. MOre Spanish lessons and a tour of Point Beach Nuclear Plant. I had a very nice host family here. I bought a dress at Filene's when we were in Boston and I wore it when I was here. It was a pretty black, Swiss dot with a lace collar. I still have it and it still fits - though a little differently. My host father presented me with $20 before leaving. Jim G. could not get over that. I assured him that his day would come too.

More cast members hometown as we continued on to Kiel, Wisconsin. Karen and Jerry K. are from here. We had "E-lympics", a bratwurst fry with the families, a tour of Lake to Lake cheese factory and much to Mark's delight, a tour of a farm. We had more Spanish lessons and a swing choir for greenroom.

Cedarburg, Wisconsin was our next stop. We toured the Milwaukee Pabst Brewery. Mark McGrath prepared the cast dinner.

June 30th, - We traveled to Green Bay, Wisconsin. We did a show at the Wisconsin Maximum Security Prison. We also did mall shows. We celebrated Canadian Dominion Day at dinner. Then we did a show at Carlton West Dinner Theatre.

July 2, 1979 - Semester Break. Half of the Cast goes home. The other half did a show for the ABC executives in Washington, D.C. I was looking forward to going home. I couldn't wait to see everyone.

Thus ended the first half of my year Tour with the singing and dancing group" Up With People".

PART III

Second Semester Up With People

It was very good to see my family when I returned home for my semester break. Grampa, however, had a surprise for me. He wanted to take me to Montreal. Now I love Montreal, but I was kind of hoping to stay put before having to leave again. I enjoyed seeing my mother and father - all my sisters and brothers, Gramma; my aunts and uncles - pretty much everyone in town. Patricia even came and spent some time with us. I loved Saint Mary's and the Sisters and Father Salmon, Father O'Reilly. Going away just really made me appreciate everything and everyone all the more.

Grampa and I did venture up to Montreal though. It is a great city and we really enjoyed ourselves. We went to a soda fountain and had ice cream sodas. The lady got a big kick out of grampa. She took our picture. I have it framed. We did a lot of walking in Old Montreal. I found this wooden mountain man - carved with snowshoes on his back and a walking stick. It reminded me of Grampa - so, gladly, I have this souvenir.

July 29th, 1979, Cast 'E' reconvened in Putnam Valley, New York. Grampa drove me down. Patricia and I stayed with Edwin's family. Edwin traveled with us the first semester but he was not going to be with us for the second semester. Several cast members were not returning for one reason or another. Kerry was getting married. In fact, Grampa and I took another trip and we stopped outside of Concord, New Hampshire to bring Kerry a wedding gift. I picked out something in crystal for her.

We learned the show in Spanish. Dino Narizzano spoke to the cast. Mr. Blatant Belk, UWP President came to visit along with Jose Rios, Mr. and Mrs. Martin and, Grampa! It was hard to say good-bye to Grampa again.

August 8th, half of the cast traveled to Montvale, New Jersey. Mr. Joe Nazarro, oru sponsor, gave a program on bullfighting. Mr. Arthur Rosen, V.P. of Gray Advertising in New York, spoke to the cast. There was a cast picnic and swimming. Helena hurt her ankle.

Viva Espana!

August 9th, Out of New York, half of the cast boarded a DC- 10 for Spain - Talavera de la Reina. I remember sitting on the plane. It seems that there had been a recent plane crash involving a DC-10. Jackie Richards looked over at me and said, "They are really safe now Virginia." The plane was huge. And it was packed.

We landed in Madrid and we got on a bus to Telavera de la Reina. The olive trees stick out in my mind. We arrived at this place where we had chicken and potatoes for lunch and fruit for dessert with wine diluted to wash down. There was a big pool there and we all went swimming. It was a hot August day. I was not so sure about how I was liking this.

We had our first host family pick-up. Bernadette Lovett was rooming with me. She had this nice relaxed way about her. She was from Tralee, Ireland. Bernadette had this thick black curly hair, freckles and bluish-green eyes. She traveled with quite a bit of luggage. She reminded me of one of the pictures of Heidi on the cover of the book. We got on very well. Only, when I offered to help with dishes or something with the family, they moreless expected it from me the whole week I was there. I was doing everything - waiting on the whole family plus Bernadette besides. It never phased her. Cafe con leche and Maria biscuits for breakfasts, with a tangerine thrown in. I liked the children. They had a pool and nice home. The little girls would always clasp my arms when we went out to walk. Just thinking of it, I can smell the Maja soap and the Florida toilet water that everyone seemed to douse themselves with. I like that toilette water though, it has a lemon, citrusy scent - very clean smelling. Louise Cummins from back home used to tell me about a Spanish acquaintance who had a "greasy look" about him.

Our First Show in Spain

August 12th - the second half of the cast arrived. Father Sabrino spoke to the Cast. We had a free day in Madrid and Toledo. We also visited the Ceramic Factory in Telavera de la Reina. I have a tile with the letter 'V' on it from there. I had also picked up some ornaments from Toledo for all my brothers and sisters. They were bright and colorful. I tried to get the corresponding Saint to match their names. For example, I got Saint Joseph for Karl as his middle name is Joseph. The only thing is, these ornaments were a little bit weighty for travel. We had our first Spanish show and it went over very well. The Spaniards are impassioned people. They really know how to live. They take siestas, they work hard, they pray hard and they sing and dance with everything they have within. Their reaction to our show was something I was not prepared for. It was so beautiful. They all hold up lights, or cigarette lighters as a great many of them smoke. Then they would ask for autographs.

A day after my mother's birthday we were in Burgos which is centrally located and in the Northern part of Spain where we did our first Acoustic for the Alcalde. For Spain, we had these rust color blouses with a pin-stripe plaid print to them. The fellows had a Western look with Wranglers, and a gingham cotton shirt with collar. We also received new show costumes for our Spanish Tour. The ladies were given either soft blue, navy blue or soft green blouson peasant top with blouson-style pantalons that came just below the knees. Mine was the soft blue which pleased me as I love that color. The men wore light blue and white striped shirt with a darker blue trouser. I guess all in all, it was aesthetically pleasing to the eye amidst the glow of the cigarette lighters.

I was not in Spain a week when I found myself being accosted by a group of beggars. What was most disturbing was that they were young children.

Everyone was taking a siesta and I decided to explore the city. Anyway, I outran them. My running in high school paid off.

We traveled Northwest to La Coruna where we did an Acoustic on the beach. We did another one in a section of town that was poor. From one extreme to the other, we then dined at the summer home of the King and Queen of Spain (Juan Carlos I and Queen Sofia). Later we played soccer with the students.

Fruits of The Sea

Then it was on to Vigo which is just North of Portugal. We visited the Citroen factory where nice cars are made. Mark Day found a little piece of rubber on the ground there and he presented it to me. I have it to this day in that little pastelle tin which he also gifted me with. We took a boat rip to Cies and Cangas Islands where I ate the fruits of the sea. we had an assembly in the sports palace for over a thousand people in cangas. While in Vigo, we had a night at Nova Olympia which is the top disco in Europe.

Too much squid is all I can think of. Half of the cast got sick as we approached Pontevedra. Some of us managed a show for a nursing home here. We also visited the city's main Museum. We did a show for children from broken homes at a sumer camp.

There was a festival going on in this city and my host mother got some squid from one of the vendors. She forcibly dangled squid for me to swallow - an unpleasant experience. It's like the summer sausage - now I just can't take it. Grampa and I got sicker than dogs on summer sausage one time. He got some for Christmas. There must have been an air hole in the vacuum sealed package. We both came down with the worse case of botulism.

Let's go fly a kite - how about in El Ferrol. I used my spinnaker fabric windbreaker that Grampa got for me from Norm Thompson to make my kite. We took a boat ride around the harbor.

Who Go - Lugo

Who go, You go, we all go to Lugo, city with a wall surrounding the historical district for more than two kilometers built in the third century. Very nice and we had a free day. I went to St. Mary's Cathedral. I love this about Spain - so many beautiful churches and cathedrals. I feel right at home. Maybe I was not so sure when I first arrived, but I am definitley falling in love with this country. There are old Roman ruins in this Galician city.

The girls outnumbered the young men in the group at least by two to one. A few romances did occurr but I was blissfully ignorant for the most part. I was happy though, when one of the technical crew, Mitch, singled me out in presenting our mascot, this stuffed Teddy bear to me during a greenroom.

Santiago de Compostela

September 5th brought us to the great pilgrimage city of Santiago de Compestela in Northwestern Spain. This place is so special. It is vibrant - filled with life - one could hear the Tuna players or singing troubadors in the streets; both young and old and many pilgrims making their way to the culmintion of their journey, which my friend Pat Devaney might tell you, is the beginning of another. This goes back to the ninth century (814) when the Tomb of St. James was discovered with the big beautiful Cathedral de Santiago being consecrated in 1211 holding the remains of the Apostle St. James. The pilgrim route is much like a river system with all these roads running together to form one common route. The most popular route begins at St. Jean-du-Port near Biarritz,France. It is approximately 500 miles. There are several other routes originating in France and there is one that begins in Operto, Portugal. In addition, there are two Spanish routes, The Camino Ingles starting in El Ferrol and A Coruna and there is another 'Way' from Seville . Hundreds of thousands of pilgrims make this spiritual journey every year. It became a symbol of Christianity against Islam. Many churches, hospitals, pensions, hotels and restaurants have been built consequently. Upon completion of this 'Camino' or "Walk", a "Compostela" or "Certificate' is awarded in Latin, if the journey was made for Spiritual reasons. This is obtained in the Obradoiro Plaza Office in the Monastery facing the great cathedral.

Mrs. Dechame gave me a beautiful book on Santiago de Compostela for Christmas one year. It is something I had always hoped to do. On certain Feast days, the great Botafumeiro, a 1.5 meter censer weighing 50 kg is swung by eight men known as Tiraboleiros at a rapid speed using a pulley system. It is done on these significant days at the end of Mass. However, this ineffable honor was bestowed on our group during a ceremony on September 5th, 1979 in the Cathedral. We had a tour too.

Jose Rios spoke on Socialism in Spain. We did an acousitc for the president of Santiago University. We also did a show for the Mentally Handicapped in the Main Square. That is another thing I loved about Spain - was their plazas in every city or town. There would be a fountain in the center. I loved to go in all the shops too. I bought some castenettes and some pretty white lace socks that the Spanish girls all seemed to wear with their black patent leather shoes. I also bought a sterling silver Matador charm. I took pictures too, lots of pictures to preserve these wonderful memories. Patricia Murphy and I would sometimes slip in late for a rehearsal because we would go to a "bar" and have churros and cidre. We would also scout out the bakeries.

A city known for its hot springs, Ourense (Orense) was our next stop. There are three springs, la Burga, they gush from granite rock flowing westward in the city reaching almost boiling point not unlike the springs of Carlsbad. There is an old Roman Bridge, Ponte Vella, spanning the Minho River. There is the Cloister of St. Francis; other churches and of course the Ourense Cathedral dedicated to St. Martin. There are parks, botanical gardens, archaeological museums, and other historical buildings. We had an acoustic at an orphanage and we did a show at the sports palace.

Nestled in the mountains, in the Province of Leon, is Ponferrada lying on the Sil River. It is the last major town on the Camino before Santiago de Compostela. It is known for its Templar Castle which was a gift to the city from Ferdinand II of Leon in 1178 because the castle was used to protect pilgrims on their way to St. James. It changed hands along the way finally being incorporated to the Crown in 1486. This 16,000 square meters site was the setting for our show. It was a tricky set up of equipment. The show was pretty spectacular ensuing with fireworks.

There were of course, many beautiful churches, museums , Radio Museum and Energy Museum, and a coal-fueled power plant.

Cathedrals Galore

September 12th - Leon, Espana - Convents, Cathedrals and Basilicas are the hallmark of Leon. However, one in particular, which was built on a site of Roman Baths is the Santa Maria Cathedral: The House of Light or Pulchra de Leonina. This is a vast 1400's Gothic Cathedral with 125 stained- glass windows, plus frescoed cloisters and a museum. It is also known for its flying buttresses and towers. Saint Isidoro's built in the 10th century is of Romanesque style containing Sacred relics. It is astounding to consider all the many churches, chapels and cathedrals in this city. There are palaces in which old Spanish Royalty are entombed. There is an old part of the city surrounded by Roman- built walls. The government buildings boast Renaissance architecture. There are parks galore and palaces, art museum amongst others. There is even a casino. This is the largest city and the capital city of Leon province in Northwestern Spain and it is on the Bernesga River. We did a show at a pensionista. We met with the Mayor and also with a Communist representative and a Socialist Representative.

Having traveled over three hours through some beautiful mountains in the Asturias Region, we arrived in the Northern city of Oviedo. Most of the Iberian Peninsula was Moorish until the invasion of Pelagius in 685 - 737. The Visigothic aristocrat revolted against the Muslims. In 720, the Moorish presence in Iberia was subsiding. They ignored this economically poor region of Astura which was uninhabited at the time. Two monks, Maximus and Fromestanus, founded the city of Oviedo in 761. A small church dedicated to St. Vincent was built here. A lot of tumultous history occurred with the city being sacked and pillaged by the Moors and then later King Alfonso I exerted his Goth influence with quite a dynasty to follow. Oviedo today is a charming medieval city.

We met the president of UNICEF and his daughter. We had rehearsal and later our show in the Bull Ring.

GORP

Many of our snacks on the road consisted of GORP - Granola, oats, raisins and peanuts. Sometimes chocolate would be added. Boy Scouts used to take "Gorp" on their hikes to sustain them. We had yogurt too. I first became acquainted with Nutella while in Spain. It would be put on this rich yellow cake - sort of like a pound cake or, it was put on those Maria plain biscuits - which are like a round flat cookie/cracker.

We did a show in the sports palace in the nearby Northern Coastal city of Gijon on September 15th. This is the largest city in the autonomous Asturian Region. It is located on the Bay of Biscay. It is known for its maritime history and the old fishermen's quarters of Cimadevilla. The beautiful St.Lorenzo Cathedral is right beside the San Lorenzo beach. Santa Catalina Hill has a clifftop park and sculpture. The eighteenth century Revillagedo Palace houses an international arts center. It adjoins the collegiate church of San Juan Bautista, now a concert hall. Nearby is the 16th century clock tower with a museum in it.

In a land that once belonged to the sea, we arrived at the third largest Asturian town of Aviles. It is also the flattest. We did a show on a soccer field and we had a free day in Oviedo. It has a national seaport and it is an industrial city. There are popular beaches there and famous churches such as St. Thomas of Canterbury. Queen Letizia is from Oviedo.

We had another show in a bullring in Zamora. Zamora is the capital of Zamora province in the Castille and Leon region in Northwest Spain. Its city center lies on the bank of the Douro River encircled by well-preserved walls and gates. The Zamora Cathedral, Bridge, and Castle are the highlights here. There is also a cloister with a museum.

Salamanca

While we performed in bullrings, we watched our first bullfight in Salamanca (complements of Jose Rios). Salamanca is known for its great sandstone architecture with intricate carvings. It boasts two cathedrals that are awe-inspiring. The great University of Salamanca is here founded in the 1100's. It was quite an intellectual center during the 1500s and 1600s and we were fortunate enough to tour it. The city dates back to the Celtic era. We did a show in the Baroque style Plaza Square where there are many cafes and restaurants and shops. There was a huge parade when we were there. Sadly, afterward, we witnessed a pedestrian being struck by a vehicle. I will never forget. I was walking alongside Julie H. from Pennsylvania. She was eating an apple. There was a lot of traffic and the cars go so fast and then without stopping. We were stunned.

We were in Salamanca for three days. My host family lived in an apartment in the city. They were an older couple. They seemed to adopt me and they wanted me to call them "Mama" y "Papa". They took me by the hand when we went out for our walks. Our sell-out show in this city was dedicated to Mrs. Martin. I believe that she was on the board of UWP. For our speaker, we had the very talented musician Dave Grossman speak on Judaism.

Mama y Papa had a hard time saying good-bye, but I have kept in touch with them. I even returned to visit them several years later.

Next stop on the tour known as "Viva la Gente" in Spain was Plasencia. This is a city in Western Spain, not far from Portugal. Of course there is The Old Cathedral built in the 1300's in a Romanesque style, and the New Cathedral built in the 1500's with Gothic and Renaissance elements. The old one is surrounded by walls - like you would see around a castle. There is an acqueduct here. There is also a unique bell tower with a clock in it in the Plaza de Mayor. Wht is unusual about it, is there is a figure of a person next to the clock. The figure is hanging on toa spiral and it looks very lifelike. Never mind the clock, that struck me. We had a picnic with our host famillies in the nearby Parque los Pinos where there were flamingos, storks and nice ponds. A little bit farther North, in Monte Valcorchero, there are cork trees and rocky trails. Lisa Ras., one of the vocal coaches, sprained her foot. I enjoyed my host family in this town. The mother worked in a factory where they made these wallets. She gave me a half dozen of them. Some had American cartoon designs on them. They had a lot of clementines too. They had sweet children and I would come "home" after the show for some tortilla. The Spaniards were great for feeding us. If one did not feel well, the host mother would prepare hot chamomile tea with honey and milk.

My grandmother would have loved it here. She always orders flan for dessert back home. We have flan here on a regular basis!

Extremadura

Anyway, our show was in a theatre in Plasencia - a first for us in Spain. We were learning new songs - "Extremadura" songs.

Now we were in the Extemadurian Region, in Navalmora de la Mata. It is a municipality in the Province of Caceres in Western, Spain. Here we saw the oldest dictionary in the world. We also toured the Almaraz Spanish Nuclear Plant which was built in 1972 with some opposition. It did boost the economy which had grown stagnate. In 1930, The Tobacco Fermentation Center was built boosting the economy. Navalmora's economy grew after the Spanish Civil War as they joined the Republican cause not wishing to be dominated by landowners. Another great thing for this city was the construction of the Valdecanas Reservoir, enabling use of the Tagus River and thus improving the population of the area. I had a great fondness for this city.

We finished out the month of September in Caceres, a city in Western Spain's Extremadura Region. It was founded by the ancient Romans though there is widespread evidence of a variety of cultures having existed there. The medieval city has fortified houses with the tiled roofs,and palaces; cobbled streets with the old town having a mix of Gothic and Renaissance architecture. What stands out most in my mind around this 12th century walled city built by the Moors, are the thirty tall towers. One can see storks nexting in them. We met with the Mayor and with a Delegate from Portugal. We went swimming at a club. We had a packed Assembly in the plaza after a parade. Half of the cast went to a Fair while the other half traveled doing assemblies.

Next day, my grandmother's birthday - October 1st. We got a free day in Elvas, Portugal. I bought all my sisters these beautiful brocade scarves/shawls in a shop there. Unfortunately, I packaged them up with the ornaments from Toledo, and the silver Matador charm and those wallets that the lady in Plasencia gave me, along with all my film to be developed. One of the cast members was staying with an American family abroad who offered to post things for the cast. We only had to give ten dollars. There were three separate shipments. My souvenirs would be going out in the third shipment. However, they never arrived. The hardest part was losing the film as I had so many treasured memories in the pictures that I had taken. I contacted my castmate and he assured me that he gave the right address and everything. Sadly, this cast mate has died. God rest Lalo. He always wore that Ralph Lauren cologne. He was a very sweet young man.

Merida

Founded by the Romans in the 1st Century B.C., is Merida, the capital of Spain's Exremadura Region. Remains of the ancient city include the still-used today 24 B.C. Teatro Romano, which has a double tier of columns onstage. Now we had done shows in bullrings, theatres, and even a castle, but we performed in this Unesco Heritage site which was a thrill above any. The ancient Punte Romano is still in use today too. This is a 792 meter bridge spanning the Rio Giadiana adjoining the Alcazaba, a 9th century fortress built over Roman walls. In all of Spain, Merida hosts the most extensive and impressive Roman Ruins. There is also a church dedicated to a young virgin martyr named Eulalia. She was only 13, a Roman Christian girl who suffered persecution (martyrdom) during the reign of emperor Diocletian. St. Eulalia pray for us

Traveling South to a town situated in the Province of Badajoz is Zafra, the capital of the comarca of Zafra - Rio Bodion. This is a most enchanting town sheltered by the Sierra Castellar Mountain range. What makes it so charming is the colored, decorative tilework on the outside of the arched walls, The streets are cobble stone. There are lots of Palm trees, outdoor cafes, music in the streets, balconies lined with flowers, shutters on tall windows that close for siesta. There is the bell tower in the town square. It is old world at its best. No one is rushed. Of course there is the plaza, the convent, the churches The town hosts one of the most important cattle fairs in Europe which was first held in 1453. This town has quite a history: where we are concerned, Zafra had an important part in the discovery of Ameria. The man who wrote the first treatise on Chess is from here. Also, the humanist and arbitrist Pedro de Valencia hails from here. We did a show in front of the Pink Parador Castle. We also visited the Alemendraleja Bodega Grapes to wine - where wine and olive oil fill the air. We picked grapes in the vineyard and tasted wine. I must have been inspired as I danced my heart out for the greenroom that evening.

October 5th, Badajoz, Espana. We were going to have a cast talent show, but it rained so it got canceled. Dave Grossman did entertain us with his music. We had a free day followed by a travel day with a stop in Toledo. Badajoz is known for its Moorish historic quarter with the fortresslike Cathedral of San Juan Bautista. The Alcazaba, with fortified walls overlooks the city located in the Southwestern part of Spain. Badajoz recorded the third hottest temperature on record for Spain at 117 degrees Farenheit on June 27th, 1864 and again in August of 1964.

Madrid

Next stop was to Spain's capital of Madrid. We were in this vibrant city for ten days. I was rooming with Cindy S. We hardly ever saw our host mother. She worked the third shift in a hospital or a lab. I remember when she got her paycheck as there were no groceries in the house and she went out to buy some. I felt bad - here she was working so hard. It seems like she had two teenage daughters at home and a son. She was a single mother. The apartment was a bit cold. I came down with the most awful bronchitis - chest cold. I could not stop coughing. And poor Cindy, it is no wonder she did not catch it as we shared the same bed. The more I think of it, I think it was our hostmother's bed as she was gone at night. I did have one host mother who gave up her bed for me. That broke my heart. These people are so selfless and they give you their best. I was hoping to room with Patricia. It seems she was in more of a suburb. Well, the first day here, we toured the ABC newspaper. Then we went to the Museo del Nacional Prado where we viewed 12th to 19th Century masterpieces of Valazquez, Goya and El Greco. Have always appreciated fine art. El Greco leaves me without words. Though there is a familiarity in the eyes of his subjects; reminds me of my father.

We had a career day the next day. I can not for the life of me recall what I did. Am thinking that I stayed in that apartment all day as I was under the weather. The following day we visited the Palacio Real. The Royal Palace of Madrid is the official residence of the Spanish Royal Family at the city of Madrid, but it is only used for official ceremonies. The Palace has 135,000 meters of floor space and contains 3,418 rooms. It is the largest royal palace in Europe. Construction began in April of 1735. It is truly too much to fathom. There is so much grandeur and opulence; fine art, antiques, sculptures, monumens, tombs, marble, Oriental carpets, china, wine cellar, root cellar - I just can not begin to describe it. And the stately grounds - the manicured lawns, and gardens, fountains. There is even The Temple of Debod which was donated by Egypt in 1968 as a sign of gratitude for Spain's help in saving the Abu Simbel Temples. It was dismantled and re-assembled in the Parque del Oueste near the Royal Palace of Madrid.

Later, we heard a speaker from the American Embassy. We did an Acoustic at a school for the deaf.

The next day brought us to another jaw-dropping place - The Royal Seat of San Lorenzo de El Escorial commonly known as the Monastery of San Lorenzo. It is a historical residence of the King of Spain approximately 45 kilometers Northwest of Madrid. This is a World Heritage Site. We also visited the Valle de Los Caidos, The Valley of the Fallen which is located in the Sierra de Guadararma eight miles North of El Elscorial. This is an impressive monument Franco commissioned to commemorate all those on both side of the Spanish Civil War (1936 - 1939). It was built between 1940 and 1958. It is a burial ground containing the remains of 33,872 Fallen on both sides along with Franco and Antonio Prima de Rivera in the crypt of the Basilica. There is a still a bit of controversy between the conservatives recognizing it as a reconciliatory act on the part of Franco, while the Regionalists, Basques and Catalans, recognize it more as a Francoist Mausoleum.

We also visited La Almudena Cathedral in Hapsburg, Madrid. The Neo-Gothic church was being built in 1879 though there was talk of construction 200 years prior. It is dedicated to the Virgin whose portrait was hidden in the wall when there was a Moorish invasion. El Cid, the famous Christian warrior, is said to have found the Image. It is said that The Virgin helped him retake the city. Itt took over 100 years to complete. The late Pope John Paul II consecrate it in 1993 when it was completed. It is next to the Royal Palace. By European standards, this is a new Cathedral though it looks old.

In between taping shows for Madrid TV, we were touring around. One day we went to Segovia and saw the great Acqueduct with 167 tall arches. We also visited the Alcazar or castle in Segovia. It is truly magical. It is said that this is the one Walt Disney used as his model for The Magic Kingdom. I made my three wishes in the striking late Gothic Segovia Cathedral lined with 1300's stained glass windows, chapels and museum. My mother always taught us to make three wishes anytime we entered a church for the first time. At the rate I was going in Spain, I was needing to dream up more wishes!

We had a show for the Minister of Culture. We did our set-up and strike from the roof tops! We had an Acoustic for the American School in Madrid. We toured the ABC newspaper publishing plant. We visited the renown Prado Museum steeped in Art history.

While in Madrid, Patricia and I scouted out a "peluqueiria" or "Hairdressers". We went where students were learning to cut hair. Here, we got our hair done - only Patricia did not like the big curls she got.

Guadalajara, an Arabic name, meaning "Stony River", is a satellite town outside of Madrid. It was part of the Moorish Kingdom of Toledo until the reign of Alfonso VI, until it was conquered by El Cid. Then in the 14th century, the Mendoza family was a strong presence here as can be noted on the Palacio del Infantado. And of course, there was a zoo, churches, parks, plazas, convents, museums. There was also a disco. We seem to get carte blanche on the discos in all the cities. They were very big in the 1970's.

Baked Alaska

One special memory, I have, is that of going to a little place to eat called "Baked Alaska". My host family took me after a show. Oh how I enjoyed the Neopolitan ice cream topped with "mile high" baked meringue on a layer of chocolate cake. It left such an impression on me, that I was to return here years later to "re-visit" this delight. Sadly, the place was not there. I think my grandfather on my mother's side said that you could not go back to a memory. He was kind of right. I mean, sure, make a new memory, but don't expect an old memory to revive itself in the same manner as it did originally. I have often thought of that.

Thursday, October 18, 1979 the cast split up into three groups as the Governor, the Mayor and the Diputacion wanted to meet us. The Diputacion gave me a little book on Guadalajara and he signed it, "Con un affection" . Later, our host families picked us up at a nursery school. We had a free evening with them. Patricia was rooming with me. We were both sick. I had seen a doctor. He told me to rest up. We went to the pharmacy the next day after lunch. I recognized a lady I had met last night who worked there. She gave me my prescription medicine free. The people are so giving and good here.

We returned to the same nursery school where 240 children aged two to six attend. We were given a tour. Then we made our way to the Plaza de Toros to set up staging. 12:45, we loaded up in the buses and went to "Las Galleras" for lunch which consisted of: soup, beefsteak with vegetables, desert, bread and water. 2:15 p.m., we loaded up again on the buses and returned to the Plaza de Toros where we had our "Current Events" discussion. 3:30 - rehearsal; 5:30, grocery dinner prepared by the Nutrition committee. 7:00 p.m. - Greenroom; 7:30 p.m. - Showtime; 10:30 p.m., Strike and interview for potential candidates for UWP. Midnight - host pick up and then Disco (optional).

"Stony River"

Patricia and I did not go to the disco. I am so klutzy. My bottle of medicine broke and smashed all over the place. Messy, Messy, Messy! Then, as I got ready for bed that night, I managed to knock a picture off the wall. I continued the mayhem in my sleep as I had a nightmare and cleared off a whole shelf of books and figurines. A combination of not feeling well and being overtired contributed to this. Fortunately, nothing broke. Then, in the morning, I brushed against the drawer of the desk, and Crash, everything fell onto the floor. My host sister rushed in. Well, I did not think much more could happen until I accidentally knocked the hoola hoop off the wall where it was hanging taking the nail with it. On top of that, I inadvertently locked myself in the bathroom and I had to get out through the bathroom window. Luckily, we have a veranda off the 7th floor! My deodorant falling on the floor and breaking was nothing at this point. I am still in Guadalajara - which incidentally means "Stony River"!

Also, after that trip to the "farmacia", Patricia and I snuk to a super market to get some "Nocilla" and some muffins to put it on. Nocilla is like "Nutella" only that was unheard of back home at that time. Our host-sister Alicia prepred us some "Manzanilla", an apple tea, which we took to our room to have with our newly acquired stash. Then the phone rang and it was for me. Alicia came into the room while we had chocolate in our mouths, It was one of those "slapstick" kind of a days. My cough was still hard. Thank goodness for the laughter - it really is the best medicine.

City of Lovers

Next stop on the tour was Teruel, the "City of Lovers". It is the original "Romeo & Juliet" story a true love story ending tragically in the 13th Century involving the wealthy Marcilla and Segura families. Diego Marcilla's family fell on hard times. He had promised since childhood to marry his sweetheart Isabel Segura. However, her father forbade it and he gave him five years to re-gain his wealth. If he did, in that allotted time, then he could have Isabel's hand in marriage. Five years to the day, Isabel's father had her married off to a Don Pedro of Azagra from Albarracin. Meanwhile, outside the church during the ceremony there was a lot of commotion. Diego had returned with great riches and the intent to marry his Isabel. However, since she had already made the vows to Don Pedro, she could not. Diego pleade with her for one kiss. This too she could not give. This was too much for Diego to bear. With a sigh, he breathed his last and died at the feet of Isabel. Then, the next day, at Diego's funeral, Isabel walked up the aisle in her wedding dress to give her true love the kiss that she refused him. Upon doing so, she collapsed prostrate on the man she loved and died. Today, one can visit their mausoleum in the Church of San Pedro.

One of our numbers in our show was "La Jota". It is the regional song and dance of this region where we were at now. Interestingly, our costumes were the most similar to theirs though they have had troupes from all over the world.

Teruel is also noted for its cured ham. The climate is dry and with an altitude of 920 metres above sea-level combined with the cold winter, making it ideal to cure the hams naturally giving it a unique flavor. Supposedly, it is the best ham in all of Spain.

This was one of my favorite places in all of Spain. Romance, history and I stayed with a lovely lady who worked with the handicapped. It was also in the autumn which is my favorite season. The leaves were a lovely gold color in the tree-lined streets. The Mudejar architecture which combines Moorish and Christian styles is most impressive with the use of ceramics and masonry. Indeed, it not only stands alone in its style for the region of Aragon, but for all of Spain. Also, dinosaur remains have been discovered here.

Since we were in the 'City of Lovers', our cast decided to have a mock Valentine's Day. We all were given a "Secret Lover". I was Jackie Richards from Yuma, Arizona . He sent me two kisses by way of one, Frank Birr, and two, Camillo who resembles Johnny Mathis. Camillo is from Argentina. Jackie, who is a fun-loving, dynamic fellow to begin with, also lavished me with a small bouquet of flowers. He had one of the music coaches deliver it to me. It was a well-kept secret! I had Jim Grigsby for mine. Jim is one of my favorites in the group. He hails from Texas. He always had his satellite radio with him and he would listen to Rush Limbaugh. I gave Jim a half of a 'Suchard' chocolate bar and half of a yellow cake that my host mom made. It was great fun.

There is also an unusual favorite pastime here. Each weekend, carloads of families, with buckets and knives, go to the country to pick "rebollones" - a kind of delicious mushroom. Families make an outing of it particularly on a nice day packing a picnic. We got to partake in this adventure searching for these delicacies. I love mushrooms anyway.

Souvenirs

October 23rd, 1979 - Logrono, Espana   We toured a candy factory where we given lots of samples of carmel and different flavored candies. I had saved my bag of candy to bring home for a gift. I picked up a bota bag in Logrono which is in Northern Spain. It is a stop on the pilgrimage to Santiago. I would pick up little charms along the way of our tour. I picked up all the states we toured and then I got a nice matador and a bull in Madrid. I had these and these gorgeous scarves/shawls from Portugal and these wallets that a host family gave me along with at least six rolls of film all put into a box to be shipped back home. Oh, and I had the white ceramic ornaments from Toledo too - what was it my great-grandmother used to"Blessed be nothing". The box never made it. The hardest part was losing the pictures as I had pictures of all my hostfamilies and of the cast members. I often think that a mail bag with mail from over forty years ago will arrive like on one of those mystery shows. Wouldn't that be something!

The Bull in the Ring

The cast members were growing increasingly more familiar and comfortable with each other. Some were restless and others had grown more yielding. That one fellow in the beginning who gave me a hard time, was now a bosom buddy. In fact, he shared something rather humorous if bawdy with me. It is amazing what fatigue and an exhausting schedule can do to one. It was constant on the go, except, it was a "no-go" for one cast member until Pamplona. We were performing a show in a bullring, and I think I went to the bathroom right beforehand. Well, well - someone must have been dancing up a storm after this number in the toilet. I have never seen anything like it to this day. And it was not going anywhere. I was astonished by the sheer size of this. I didn't want anyone to associate me with this "monstrosity". Well, it seems Jude had to use the toilet and when he came out, it was evident that he too had seen "It". Our paths crossed and it was too good to not say anything - so he shared what he saw with me. He said, and I will never forget it, "Virginia, you could put sugar on that and go skiing!" That was it for me. I could not keep my composure during the show or the rest of the evening and even now, when I think about it - I am in hysterics. I did write home and tell Grampa about it. He got a kick out of it too.

Huesca

Huesca in Northeastern Spain was the next city on our tour. It was occupied by the Moors for 800 years. After the Spanish Catholics pushed them South, the French moved into the empty city. There were Cathedrals, abbeys, museums, parks, castles and tombs to greet us. The fortifications still stand. Most impressive to me, was the Sanctuary of de

Toreciudad - a beautiful Shrine. It is tranquil and the views are superb. We had a presentation on the city of Huesca at the Ministry of Culture center. The cast had to have vaccinations which caused quite a stir. We had our usual routine set-ups and strikes at the Diputacion, school and our show venue otherwise.

After siesta on a free day, my host family, had some sort of an electric warmer under the table which was draped with a heavy cloth. We sat around rolling dates in sugar, and eating roasted chestnuts. This is such a sweet recollection for me.

We did an assembly at a hospital in Zaragoza after first having a reception with the Vice- President Jose Luis Merino. We also visited the renown "Opus Dei Retreat Center". This was founded by Father Jose Maria Escriva. His motto was to divinize work in the every day work field. He was a retreat master.

We had a show at the Sports Palace in addition to an Assembly at the hospital where we would go in the rooms and talk with the patients. This was most gratifying. We had to make sure our host families had their tickets for the show as we would not go home with them until after the show. We also made sure to eat "seconds" at lunch as we would not have a snack before the show as we typically did. There were dressing rooms and showers, to stage right for the ladies, and stage left for the gents. Then "Sala de Verde" - green room before the show.

The next day, after our "Current Events", we departed to the Peking Restaurant for Chinese food. Patricia, Mark and I sat together. We enjoyed improvising with the chopsticks. Later we returned to the Sports Palace for rehearsal with Billie Chan. After our second show in this city, we had a surprise: "Strike Food"! The Air Force Base brought in food for us all to eat and it was American.

Catalan

In the Catalan Region of Northeastern Spain is the city of Lerida founded in the third century B.C. It became a Roman town in 80 B.C. It was a city used for strategic and Military purposes. Julius Caesar and his troops inhabited the city in the year 49 B.C. It was invaded by the Muslims and then King Ramon Berenguer recaptured it and King James the 4th later governed the city. Later on it was invaded again, in 1707 until the Spanish Civil War. Then it recovered and developed into an agricultural center and a growing textile industry. The city is on the banks of the Serge River in the Pyrenhees Mountains. It is great for winter sports. This city appealed to me very much. There is, however, one experience that has left an unsavory memory, That was when my host family took me to where a cow or bull was being butchered. The family was getting fresh blood sausages - something that I always liked until I witnessed this. Other than that, our cast had a "Secret Pumpkin Time" and a costume party. The costume that stands out the most in my mind, is that of one fellow from the Philadelphia area. His name was Nate. Nate wore a diaper and carried a rattle. Then, our show was in the "Crystal Palace". It was a benefit for ASPROS - an organization that helps the mentally handicapped. Oh, and since it was Halloween, our logistics team arranged for a nighttime tour of the Cathedral. When lit up, it gives the illusion of floating. Some notable foods in this region are marinated clams, eels, snails, quail, rabbit, mussels, tomato marmalade and the blood and bone marrow sausages!

Andorra

From All Hallows Eve to All Saints Day, we then loaded up on the two buses and headed for one of my most favorite places I have ever seen. That is, Andorra, the sixteenth smallest country in the world - or the eleventh smallest if one goes by population. It is located between France and Spain high up in the Pyrenhees. It is owned by two countries. The President of France governs it along with the Bishop of Urgell in Catalonia, Spain. It is believed that Charlemagne created this Principality. Patricia and I enjoyed roaming the winding streets in the mountains. The colors were brilliant. We scouted out bakeries and candy shops. I bought a huge "Cote d'or" chocolate bar. It was duty-free as are all the goods in this little country. That was the best chocolate I have ever had. It had a red wrapper with an elephant design on it. Patricia and I then took pictures. My film got lost but I do recall that I was wearing a red, yellow and green plaid skirt with a red vest and a green turtleneck shirt. I was holding a French newspaper and wearing my new black Basque beret trying to blend in with the background. The setting reminded me of Heidi which is one of my all-time favorite books.

Valencia

Next, a little over a five hour bus ride took the cast the the third largest city on the East Coast of the Iberain Peninsula. Valencia lies on the shores of the Turia River of the Mediterranean. It is one of the most beautiful and historical cities in the world renown for its fairs and avant garde architecture. It is a lively center for commerce and business worldwide. Orange trees abound and that wonderful saffron rice dish with seafood known as "Paella" hails from here.

My host family must work in the orange groves as they had lots and lots of oranges. The "Valencia" Orange hails from California though. My host mother made this delicious yellow pound cake using olive oil. She served it with cafe con leche.

We visited the "Lladro Factory" here. One cast member, Nate, purchased many statues to take back home. I had a little money from the sell of our records. I got a statue of a slender girl holding a stack of books. This would be for my mother as she is a librarian. This was a "Nao" statue which was a division of Lladro and not quite as expensive - but just as beautiful in the sleek pale blue and brown color on the smooth porcelain.

We had a reception with the Mayor of Valencia and with Sister Fernando Martinez Castellanos. I have come across that name only one time before and that is with the Episcopalian priest at my paternal grandmother's church in Ticonderoga - Reverend Kermit Castellanos. We then departed for the Parque los Viveros for rehearsal. We did a couple of shows there.

One of our cast staff members was from Wales. Her name is Gill and her father worked for Scotland Yard. He was visiting his daughter at the time.

It was arranged that he come and enlighten us on the legal system in England. Besides the wonderful Welsh accent, it was very interesting. Lunches were at Sacis Restaurant for several days while in Valencia.

We also had a tour along the Harbor of La Albufera. This is the most important arice area in Spain. We visited a "Barraca", a typical house of the Valencian farmer. Later, we sailed by boat along the picturesque lake. We returned to Valencia later that night of November 5th.

The next day was a free day to take in the Central Market, or the Bull Fighting Museum, the Museum of History, but without compare and ....

If you are searching for "The Holy Grail", search no further. Eureka! It is here in the Cathedral of Valencia in the Chapel Santo Caliz. It is the One used by Our Lord Jesus Christ during The Last Supper. It was originally in Antioch and eventually found its way to Valencia after the reconquest. Saint Joseph of Arimethea also collected The Blood of Jesus on The Cross in this Chalice. Hearing the Gregorian Chant rise to the vaulted ceiling is ineffably beautiful in a place that transcends all.

Palma de Mallorca

That night, we took a twelve hour overnight boat trip to the Balearic Island of Palma de Mallorca. It was magical watching the sun rise as we were coming into port. Rick from California came up to admire the sunrise. Shortly after, we went to the palace de Deportes Carreera. Our host families picked us up at 1:00. Later we would return for rehearsal and a 'grocery" dinner, greenroom, show and pick up. I was staying with a family that had a gorgeous home on a cliff overlooking the sea. The lady was glamorous who lived there. She had a son, a "muy guapo" son, who brought me back to rehearsal on his motorcycle. Host pick up was 11:30 that night. It was standard to be that late in Spain as the days started later, lunch or dinner rather, was served at 1 or 1:20 followed by a siesta where everything closed down in the cities. It was a laid-back lifestyle with family at the core. I liked it. I liked Spain.

The next day, Patricia and I were in our glory as we discoverd the famed 'Ensaimada' Pastry. This is a flaky delicate coil-shaped pastry dusted in confectioner's sugar. It is believed to be from the Middle East. It can be filled with pumpkin jam or almond nougat or be plain. It is often served with coffee for breakfast or as a snack with a sweet plant-based drink known as "horchata". This is made from 'chufas' or tiger nuts. It is a sweet, white frothy drink.

Now for that "Pearl of great price" - we departed for the Pearl Factory of Manacor. We got to see how the Mallorcan pearls are made. This is a unique and delicate process of organic pearls that's end result mirrors that of cultured pearls. They are exquisite. It had now become my mission to bring one of these beauties home to my mother. I selected a beautiful grey tear drop shaped pendant. It was in a velvet lined red box. It would easily fit in my travel bag too. I noticed Nate got several Mallorcan Pearl pieces.

It is so much fun to embrace a culture and to take a little piece of something from a place that has special meaning - indeed a souvenir!

It just kept getting better. Next on the itinerary, was a visit to the Caves of Puerto Cristo Caves of Drach or "Dragon" Caves. This was ethereal. We took a boat ride and the lights shining on the stalacites were magnificent. The colors would make one think of the Aurora Borealis. Then, out of the depths, the most beautiful Classical music sounded. This is something I would love to go back and experience. Yet the memory is as brilliant as yesterday.

One of the castmembers, a fellow, seemed to resent that my host brother was dropping me off on the motorcycle. I still don't know why but it is something I sensed. Same as when I got my new Basque beret, I felt some old men in one of the Plazas were making fun of me. Probably because the hat is primarlly worn by men even though women don berets in Scotland and such. Another feeling that I felt was when our cast had free time at one of the beaches and several of the fellows made sure that I arrived back to the bus alright. I suppose they were looking out for me -

was not quite sure. I had a tendency to wander around full of wonder. Perhaps they sensed something that I did not. Grampa was always saying that I was so "G-- Da-n naive"!

We had several shows in Palma. Our sponsor was ASPACE which is an association that helps children with Cerebral Palsy.

Our castmates from Bermuda arrangeda Bermuda-style dinner while in Palma.

We had a free day on Sunday, November 11th. I went to Mass, wrote home and went to the beach with my host family. On the 12th, we boarded the boat at Parque del Mar and made our way back to Valencia.

We spent a night in Valencia and the next day we traveled to Madrid. We had a filming of a TV special at RTV Espana. Get out the Max Factor Pancake number two. One of our cast members, Beth, from Colorado had a surprise visit from her family in the states.

We were also presented with a baby lion!

The Zoo in Madrid

On one free day while in Madrid, I went out exploring. I ended up at the Zoo in Madrid. It was magical. I was enchanted seeing all the exotic animals and I felt unencumbered just on my own. As the day drew on, I felt that I was being observed. This young man with dark hair and dark eyes seemed to be not far from wherever I was. He approached me and introduced himself to me - Jose was his name. He asked if I would like to join him for the mid-day meal. What was to stop me. So we had dinner at the restaurant in the Zoo. It was very nice and I enjoyed this adventure. I returned to my host family with a zoo button that I have long wanted to give to a gal in the group named Kim. She collects buttons such as these. I would find it and then misplace it again, but it is still earmarked for her.

Mid-November 1979 brought us to Castellon, a beautiful province just North of Valencia on the Mediterranean Coast. We had a bonfire on one of the breathtaking beaches and Kentucky Fried Chicken of all things!

The next day the fellows in our Cast surprised the gals with breakfast. Jerry from Wisconsin was the waiter for Patricia, Diane and myself. Following this, we had an acoustic for the governor, mayor and president with a small group. Mid-day dinner was at China Restuarant and we performed for 11,000 in a bullring that night. We had a sell-out show the next night too in the same venue. UNICEF was our sponsor.

Manuel and Pepe

The next city on our tour was exciting because it is home to our two bus drivers to whom we were all growing very attached: Manuel and Pepe. They have been with us ever since we first set foot on Spanish soil. They really cared for us and they enjoyed being with us. Murcia is their city. This city is known as the "Orchard of Europe" because of its temperate climate all year round. The Arabs converted this region into a rich land by an irrigation system which is still in use today. It is one of the most important agricultural centers in the country. It is the seventh largest city in Spain. The Coast is a 45 minute drive away and the beautiful Fuensante Mountains rise majestically only six kms. away.

Kelly from Massachusetts was rooming with me. She was growing very homesick and our host family so kindly let her call home on their telephone. I called my family as it was Thanksgiving time but I called 'Collect'. The Spaniards would give the shirt off their backs even when they have nothing.

We did our show in front of the Cathedral. It rained. More disturbing was seeing young people sniffing glue.

Thanksgiving

Willis organized our Thanksgiving dinner. We all brought in a food item to help the poor people in this region. We did an acoustic the next day and we did a show in a bullring the next night.

Alhama de Murcia which is in the Province of Murcia was our next stop. It is a very small town with friendly people - sort of microcosm of what Spain is. Farming is the major influence here: oranges, lemons, olives and grapes. There is also a Pork Plant we passed as we were bussed in.

It was very neat because less than a mile from my host family, there was a small castle on the hill. It was much like walking up to Mount Defiance back home. Patricia and I made the trek late one morning. Our show was to benefit the Red Cross - to assist in building and manning an aid station on the road to Murcia. The town has one traffic light, three international telephone boothd and two discoteques. Oh, and there is a garden of the ducks! I liked the quaintnest of this town.

At the foot of the Sierra Nevada Mountains is the multi-cultural, rich in history city of Grenada. It offers skiing at 738 meters above sea level and yet it is less than an hour to the Mediterranean Coast. It is built on the confluence of four rivers. It has its University, Cathedral, and the magnificent Alhambra.

The Cast had a "Sup-e- Bowl" I was on the committe for this. I was also the mascot. We met at the city University which was donated to us for our activity, Patricia and I got into the "GORP". That afternoon at 1:40, we walked to the cafeteria for lunch. We were trying to beat the mad rush of the students coming in at 2 p.m. Anyway, for some strange reason, everyone was clanging their knives on their glasses giving yours truly the most thunderous ovation. I got this upon entering and leaving the cafeteria. Let's see, I was wearing a flared skirt with a sailor shirt, deck sneakers and white ankle socks and sporting pig tails. I don't know. It was a nice send- off as we loaded the buses to the Alhambra.

Later that evening upon host pick-up, my host sister Marie Carmen took me for a walk around the city. We visited a church which I just love to do.

The Alhambra citadel in Granada is one of the greatest buildings in Spain. It is a Moorish fortress with grand archways and delicate mosaics. I was awestruck and transported to another world in another time here. To see the Alhambra from a different vantage, we went to the Mirador of San Nicholas. This view is perhaps the most captivating in all of Spain. One can see the city of Granada with its cobblestone streets, the palatial Alhambra and the majestic mountains of the Sierra Nevada. In fact, I picked up a little round sew-on patch of the Sierra Nevada Mountains. I figured that I could sew it on a jacket or sweatshirt when I got home. It still sits in the corner of my top drawer! To quote Shakespeare, "Every inquisitive traveller keeps Granada in his heart without having even visited it."

Another city in the Andalusian Region, in the South Central part of Spain that we visited was Jaen. The name derives from the Roman Villa Gaiena which the Arabs pronounced "Jayyan". We had a travel day and our show both in the same day: "Set up! Strike! Take a Level with Lisa" were the catch phrases of the day. We still had time to take in the Santa Catalina Castle with a walk to see "La Cruz" or "The Cross". I appreciate the Spaniards and that they are not afraid to show their Faith in these wonderful monuments. One will see huge Cross monuments in Portugal and Brazil too."

My souvenir here, a bota bag. This is a leather pouch shaped like a hearth bellow with a cord for carrying around one's neck. It may hold water or wine for the thirsty. Here in Jaen, there are many streams flowing from the rugged triple terraced terrain. Hence, I had fresh water for my bota bag. Where the water flows into the lakes trout can be had. This is also the largest olive growing center in Spain with its corresponding industries.

Catch Phrases

"Let's go, Let's Show, Let's Rodeo!" This was one of my favorite heard expressions in the group. Jim from Wyoming coined that one. " We're ramblin' now" was another one; actually, any phrase with the word 'ramble' in it was a catch phrase. Jude could be overheard saying, "I love ya, get out of here." "Go for it!" and "It's historia" were others. "It's 'Secret Person Time', "Vamos", "Don't drink the water!", and "Mail, Where's the mail?!" were other popular expressions. I was overheard to exclaim, "Oh, Sugar Pops!".

One of the oldest cities in the world, founded by the Pheonicians in the 8th Century is Malaga, our next stop. It is the Southernmost city in Europe on the Costa del Sol of the Mediterranean. It is also the birthplace of Picasso. Indeed this city is brimming with art, crystal and glass exhibits, classic car shows; the Cathedral known as 'The One-Armed Lady", castles and botanical gardens. It is very popular with the tourists. More than 12 million passengers a year use its fourth largest airport in Spain here. Malaga is 100 km east of the Strait of Gibralter and 130 km North of Africa. In fact, we had an opportunity to take a hydro-plane boat to Tangiers - not for the faint of heart! We were briefed on what to expect. I got a brass candlestick and a brass spoon there. It was very interesting to see the market there. The little spoon was for my castmate Kathy who's last name happened to be "Spoon".

"Everybody ready to 'Rock and Roll'" as we prepared for our Assembly in the Paseo de Parque. "One, two, three - STRETCH!" We also did a show in nearby Torremolinos at the Convention Center. Lunch was at Ristorante Belle Napoli.

USS INDEPENDENCE

But, the real highlight of the tour for me, was our show on the aircraft carrier 'The USS INDEPENDENCE'. This was a show that was not on our itinerary per se, but rather fit in at the last moment. The Gulf War was on in The Middle East. There was a fatal helicopter crash landing earlier in the week on the USSS INDEPENDENCE. It was thought tht our music could lift the morale of our US Sailors. Thus on the last day of November in 1979, our cast met at Carranque and then made our way to the Pier. It was all kind of "hush hush". Many in the group were frightened and emotional with thoughts of war looming in their head. We were brought to the aircraft carrier via smaller boats. I can still see the big flat elevator!

It was exciting as I have never seen or been on a ship like this. We got to eat with the sailors in their 'Mess Hall'. There was American food and soft ice cream. One sort of felt like this is what it is all about. If one can lift his brother up - lift his morale, than it is a very wondrous thing. We set up to do our show that afternoon. Strangely enough, out on the Mediterranean Sea, the sound was not working. Yet, one could hear a pin drop. We sang from our hearts. We reached these men. It was the most powerful show for me in our whole year. Many eyes were wet with tears. One of the sargents took me under his wing. His name was Ron. Upon leaving, going down on that elevator, Ron tossed his hat from above, "God Bless you Virginia". I cherish that hat - that memory and yes, I do have that hat to this day on my bureau at home.

We still had a couple of more shows in this city. We had just started practicing our Christmas music and we had various conferences on living on your own and life after Up With People.

Ronda

Traveling 100 km West, and definitely not for the faint of heart for this bus journey, we went up the mountain on steep, steep, and narrow, narrow roads to Ronda where there is a thousand foot drop from the bridge. Our ride was moonlit! Pre-historic settlements, dating back to the Neolithic Age including the rock paintings of Cueva de la Pileta can be found here. The Celts were the first settlers here around the sixth Century B.C. They called it 'Arunda'. Later, Phoenecian settlers established themselves here referring to Ronda as Old Ronda. The current Ronda is of Roman origins. It has been founded as a fortified post in the second Punic War by Sipio Africanus. Julius Caesar later gave Ronda a title as city. The three bridges offer outstanding views. This city is built on top of rock formations so high up. I felt like I was on top of the world. I enjoyed the thrill of this city with its landscape or should I say hillscape!

One neat phenomenon that occurs nightly at 7 p.m., is that Venus can be visibly and clearly seen in the sky. Ronda also boats the oldest Plaza de Toros or bullring in Spain. We had our Assembly here and we did an evening show at the "Polidoportivo". In addition, the man who invented the guitar, Espinel, is from here. People from all over the world come here to view the gorge.

Huelva

We were told that there was "Huelva down the road." Huelva, 'Hail'-va - this is where Christopher Colombus hails from. He prayed to the city's Patron Saint - Our Lady, the Virgin of Cinta before making his voyage with local sailors he recruited and discovering the Americas. There is a monument in his honor here. North of the city has brought Phoenecians, Greeks, and Romans to the mineral wealth of the area. Later the Moors arrived - all leaving their mark on this city. The 1755 Lisbon earthquake damaged a lot of the city. However, there are still lovely plazas and the Cathedral de la Merced with a lovely Baroque facade standing along with the church of San Pedro. There are lots of seafood restaurants int what is said to be the "Sister City of Texas".

We visited 'La Rabida' - the Monastery where Christopher Columbus spent much of his time while preparing for his epic voyage. Interestingly, this city is referred to as "Bethlehem" or "The Cradle of the New World". More interesting, is the discovery of the existence of the "semi-mythical harbor city Tartessos on the South Coast of the Iberian Peninsula. This is mentioned in The Bible. Greeks believed that European Civilization began here. In the first millennium B.C., Herodotus describes the city as behind the Pillars of Heracles or what we know as The Strait of Gibraltar. It was an area rich in metal: true tin, copper, bronze and even gold. There was a thriving market there in the 4th Century B.C. However, in the Bible, it refers to Tartessos as more of a land of perdition. In any event, this city did actually exist.

Huelva is 30 miles from Portugal and less than 15 minutes from the beach on the Atlantic Ocean. This harbor is one of the safest and most sheltered ports in Spain as well as one of the busiest seaports in Europe..

We did two shows at the newly built Polideportivo. We did an Assembly at the Ayuntamiento where we presented Senor Jesus Bravo with a pin. We visited the Port City of Palos from where Columbus and his three ships sailed. Lunch was at the Huelva Golf Club. We had an afternoon of study with one of our staff on the team - Joy; than rehearsal, "grocery dinner", greenroom and show at 8:30.

Seville

Seville, the most charming of cities where everything balances - building seem to mirror each other. Orange blossoms abound... The 'Flamenco' dance was born here. Christopher Columbus is buried here - in the third largest Cathedral in the world. There are three universities. The city is brimming with life and palm trees. The Valley of the Guadalquivir River runs through Seville a strategic point considering that gold and silver from the New World was transported here and then distributed throughout Spain. The Alcazar Palace is here, the Giralda Tower, The Gold Tower and the magical barrio of Santa Cruz with its narrow streets. The fountains in the plaza and the Maestranza Bullring are some of what make seville so enchanting.

What piques my curiosity was the Seville orange as Grampa always had Seville Marmalade for his English muffins. The Seville orange is actually a sour or bitter orange. It had been introduced and cultivated heavily by the Moors in the tenth Century in Spain. It is a cross between a pomelo and a mandarin orange. This is what gives its marmalade that distinct tangy flavor. Citrus is a big part of the Mediterranean diet.

Christmas was in the air. I picked up some pretty Spanish Christmas cards here as well as a couple of cassettes with Spanish Christmas music. "The Sound of Music" was playing at the cinema and we could watch it for 100 pesetas if we so desired. Patricia and I went. It had Spanish captions and it always delivers.

Our shows were at the Casino de la Exposicion. We had a nice lunch at the Hostera del Prado at the Plaza de San Sebastian: Escalope Milanesa with spaghetti, water, and for dessert - ice cream which was thrown in by the restaurant. December 8th marked our last show on the Iberian Peninsula. Ida from Norway made a Norwegian lunch that day followed by a talk with Father Sabrino. Then, we were treated to an afternoon Classical Recital. There was no admission charge for our last shows on the mainland.

You Know You Are in Spain When ....

Got thinking about some funny things in Spain with our host families. For example: You know you are in Spain if you hear a hissing sound, it is a spaniard trying to get your attention; or the next door neighbor takes the donkey to the supermarket; it takes longer to find the flusher than it did to find the bathroom; you know that you are in Spain when you are given four plates to eat your lunch on; you hear 'Benga, benga, Mira, mira from your host mother as she firmly taps you on the shoulder; your host family tells you that their house is muy cerca when it is actually two kilometres down the road all while walking with our luggage!; everyone from one to 100 smokes; they speak of places as being old and they mean thousands of years old; the toilet paper is thicker than your stationery; you take a bath in a tub smaller than a sink; your host mom goes into vivid detail trying to explain which is hot and which is cold in the shower only to find out that they are both cold; a waste basket in the house is virtually unheard of; you use a dictionary to find out what you are having for supper and then you wish that you had not looked; you look down at your lunch and it looks back!; the bruises you have are not from set up or striking the equipment, but rather from your host mom who pokes you ever time she asks you something; you take a shower at night and just as you are rinsing your hair - the water in the building shuts off!; your dressing room is where the bulls are kept after they have met with the Matador; the sides of the buses kiss the houses as they you go down the streets in them; after twenty minutes with your host family - all they wanted to do was move your chair.

I am struck by the costumes and festive dress in this city. The women have their hair pulled back- it looks shiny and they smell of Florida eau de toilette. The little girls wear black patent leather shoes with the prettiest hand chrocheted white pointelle socks. There is a lot of lovely lace in the shops.

The Canary Islands

After Mass with my host family, on Sunday, December 9th, I meet our group at the same place where we had our show the previous night. Our group departs for the Airport. We depart for Las Palmas in the Grand Canary Islands.

We arrived and met our host families. I loved mine - really I enjoyed them all. It seems my host father walked in on me in the bathroom in the middle of the night. He was more embarrassed than I was. However, I had an accident of the monthly kind catching me off guard. I was trying to wash the bedding and my night attire. My host mother was asking me what happened. I think she thought I wet the bed. But then I am sure she must have known. She seemed to be chuckling about it. So much for discretion.

Our first show here was at the Teatro Perez Galdos which is a gorgeous theatre.

The next morning we departed for Maspalomas which, of all things, is a "Nude Beach". We were instructed to stay together and not go in that part. Everyone's imagination ran wild that day. This must have been the beach where Bill and Willis were looking out for me.

We had lunch and set up and rehearsed at the Polideportiva which is another name for a Spanish Sports Center. We had our Strike (take down the stage equipment) and interviewed prospective candidates for future Up With People Casts. Host pick up was at mid-night.

The next day, on the Feast of Saint Lucy, we met at the docks and embarked on a voyage to Tenerife. We arrive at the Ferry Port and transfer our luggage to the buses. Then we have lunch at Fontana de Oro - buffet-style.

The Canary Islands have a year-round temperate climate. It is a Spanish archipelago and the Southernmost autonomous community of Spain located 100 kilometres West of Morocco at the closest point. It gets its name from the Latin "canariae insulae" - Island of dogs used by Arnobius. The inhabitants kept large dogs. However, there is a conflicting report that states a Berber from an African Tribe who was called "Canaraii" and therefore the island took his name. The bird was named after the Canary Islands - not the other way around. There is the Maritime Trade and farming and a thriving tourism that sustains the people here.

The Last Dance

We then loaded the buses for Palacio des deportes for our host pick-up. Early evening we leave for Porta de la Cruz. Sandwiches are brought in from the same restaurant where we had lunch. We have our greenroom, our show , strike and interview. We leave for La Laguna for host pick-up at 11:30 p.m. The next day is much the same. Saturday, December 15th was a free day until the evening. We were to dress up and meet at the Hotel Mency for dinner. This was our final cast banquet. It was bittersweet. Christy from Texas sang a song she wrote which was very sweet. Matt and Jill put on a comedic skit of the whole year. Awards were handed out. It seems they voted me 'Most Innocent'. However, the next night, for our very last show, I was rather mischievous. We had our last show at the Palacio. It occurred to me that I was never selected for any of the dances or songs. I was destined to remain in the background. Well, that was fine, but for just once, my good friend Mark agreed to let me step in to do the dance steps that go with "It's a Memorable Tune." The show was bursting with energy and emotion. My cast mates were cheering me on. I took this moment to shine and I owned it. The next day, one of the dance directors approached me and reprimanded me. I thought, I took the chance that was never given to me and tomorrow we are all going our separate ways. No lo siento.

We had a mid-night host pick-up. Then, at 4:45 the next morning of December 17th we would fly from Aerpuerto del Sur in Tenerife to Madrid. We would arrive in Madrid before noon and leave the airport for lunch with Senor Jose Rios and his family. Senor Rios is on the Board of Up With People. We received diplomas for finishing our year. We then went to our host families, our 88th family of the year, for one last night. 6:30 a.m. on Tuesday, December 18th we arrive at Aravaca downtown Madrid. 7:30 we depart for the airport. We arrive at 8:15 a.m. and board Spantax Flirght 991 to New York. "Be there or be square" as some of the folks would say. Odios amigoes. I would be home in time for Grampa's birthday on December 20th and to be with my family for Christmas. Thank you Lord!

"There are many roads

that come together;

they don't all go the same way

but they get there, just the same;

and I have a feeling

that we will meet once again

where the roads come together

of the way "

Herb Allen, UWP